Library Volunteers

PRACTICAL GUIDES FOR LIBRARIANS

About the Series

This innovative series written and edited for librarians by librarians provides authoritative, practical information and guidance on a wide spectrum of library processes and operations.

Books in the series are focused, describing practical and innovative solutions to a problem facing today's librarian and delivering step-by-step guidance for planning, creating, implementing, managing, and evaluating a wide range of services and programs.

The books are aimed at beginning and intermediate librarians needing basic instruction/guidance in a specific subject and at experienced librarians who need to gain knowledge in a new area or guidance in implementing a new program/service.

About the Series Editors

The **Practical Guides for Librarians** series was conceived and edited by M. Sandra Wood, MLS, MBA, AHIP, FMLA, Librarian Emerita, Penn State University Libraries from 2014–2017.

M. Sandra Wood was a librarian at the George T. Harrell Library, the Milton S. Hershey Medical Center, College of Medicine, Pennsylvania State University, Hershey, PA, for over thirty-five years, specializing in reference, educational, and database services. Ms. Wood received an MLS from Indiana University and an MBA from the University of Maryland. She is a fellow of the Medical Library Association and served as a member of MLA's Board of Directors from 1991 to 1995.

Ellyssa Kroski assumed editorial responsibilities for the series beginning in 2017. She is the director of Information Technology at the New York Law Institute as well as an award-winning editor and author of 36 books including *Law Librarianship in the Digital Age* for which she won the AALL's 2014 Joseph L. Andrews Legal Literature Award. Her ten-book technology series, *The Tech Set* won the ALA's Best Book in Library Literature Award in 2011. Ms. Kroski is a librarian, an adjunct faculty member at Drexel and San Jose State University, and an international conference speaker. She has just been named the winner of the 2017 Library Hi Tech Award from the ALA/LITA for her long-term contributions in the area of Library and Information Science technology and its application.

Library Volunteers
A Practical Guide
for Librarians

Allison Renner

PRACTICAL GUIDES FOR LIBRARIANS, NO. 62

ROWMAN & LITTLEFIELD
Lanham • Boulder • New York • London

Published by Rowman & Littlefield
An imprint of The Rowman & Littlefield Publishing Group, Inc.
4501 Forbes Boulevard, Suite 200, Lanham, Maryland 20706
www.rowman.com

6 Tinworth Street, London SE11 5AL, United Kingdom

British Library Cataloguing in Publication Information Available

Library of Congress Cataloging-in-Publication Data

Names: Renner, Allison, 1985– author.
Title: Library volunteers : a practical guide for librarians / Allison Renner.
Description: Lanham : Rowman & Littlefield, [2019] | Series: Practical guides for librarians ;
    no. 62 | Includes bibliographical references and index.
Identifiers: LCCN 2018056839 (print) | LCCN 2018059806 (ebook) | ISBN 9781538116920
    (electronic) | ISBN 9781538116913 (pbk. : alk. paper)
Subjects: LCSH: Volunteer workers in libraries—United States. | Libraries and community—
    United States.
Classification: LCC Z682.4.V64 (ebook) | LCC Z682.4.V64 R46 2019 (print) | DDC
    023/.3—dc23
LC record available at https://lccn.loc.gov/2018056839

∞™ The paper used in this publication meets the minimum requirements of American
National Standard for Information Sciences—Permanence of Paper for Printed Library
Materials, ANSI/NISO Z39.48-1992.

Printed in the United States of America

to Theo,
love kisses

Contents

Figures and Tables

⟲ Figures

⟲ Tables

Preface

Library Volunteers: A Practical Guide for Librarians is a complete handbook to starting, restructuring, or maintaining a volunteer program. Volunteers are one of the most overlooked and underused resources available to nonprofits and other organizations. This handbook will help find willing volunteers in the community and utilize their skills in a way that benefits the volunteer as well as the organization.

Overseeing volunteers can be a daunting task. On top of all of the other duties library staff are typically responsible for, creating a volunteer program from scratch can seem nearly impossible. Hiring a volunteer coordinator or allowing a specific employee to hand off library duties to other staff in order to oversee the volunteer program is ideal, and this handbook will help that person minimize the initial workload of taking on a volunteer program. With stretched budgets and endless job duties, hiring a new person or shifting responsibilities is not always possible in a library environment. With all of the background information and sample paperwork included, this handbook lightens the load for library employees kickstarting a volunteer program, even with the other duties they need to complete. Anything that can make volunteer management easier on library and nonprofit staff will benefit everyone involved.

While the language and job descriptions are specifically geared toward volunteer programs in a library setting, the information provided can easily be adapted to help any nonprofit organization take advantage of potential volunteers and utilize them in a way that will further the organization's mission. Sections on outreach and connecting patrons with volunteer opportunities beyond library walls will also benefit various community organizations in terms of potential partnerships. These sections will also help community and nonprofit organizations understand how they can work with libraries to leverage all of their resources.

The work doesn't stop once the program is created: volunteers have to be trained and retained; job duties have to be written, assessed, and refreshed; the benefits of the program need to be documented and weighed. This book covers every aspect of volunteer programs, from creating, to recruiting, to retaining and keeping the opportunities fresh and appealing. It has information pertaining to elementary age, teenage, and adult volunteers, including innovative and unique volunteer positions that can be offered to them. Also covered are both school and public library settings, but the information provided can be adapted slightly to benefit any organization that has a need for volunteer help.

This book looks beyond the scope of the library to include information on outreach and partnering with community organizations to provide volunteer opportunities to library patrons and volunteers on a broader scale. It is a complete handbook for library and nonprofit employees to use to solve any volunteer issue they might have.

After working in both public and school libraries that did not have developed volunteer programs, I thought about how I could create them, how I could bring others on board, and how it could keep running beyond my tenure. The information in this book is innovative because it provides all the background necessary to start a program but includes ways to keep the program fresh and expand it beyond the library walls, so that the volunteer program will be positioned to make an impact on the community at large, not just the library's patrons.

I began volunteering as a child and continued into adulthood; many of my volunteer experiences led to jobs within the organizations. While volunteering itself is rewarding in so many ways, having my experience valued by the organization to the extent that they were willing to pay me for what I was already doing for free was a huge compliment! After a year of volunteering for SRVS, an organization that provides resources for people with disabilities and their families, I was hired to be their first volunteer coordinator. Working with employees in Public Relations and the Learning Center for adults with disabilities, I created a quality volunteer program from the ground up. There were liability issues considering the population we were working with, and volunteers had to do fairly extensive online training and agree to background checks. I thought that would be enough to push volunteers away, but we never had a shortage of help. I learned that when people are passionate about the time and skills they have to give, they will do what they need to do in order to share that.

I volunteered at a branch of the Memphis Public Library while completing my Master of Library Science, and after graduating was hired as a teen services librarian who oversaw the teen volunteer program. At the same time, I was a volunteer blogger for the Young Adult Library Services Association's YALSAblog, then applied for and was hired as the blog's Member Manager—still a volunteer position! I could not believe how much volunteerism had factored into my life, my purpose, and even led to many different career opportunities.

I worked in the public school system as an elementary librarian and had a chance to bring in student volunteers. These students came in at the end of the day before the buses loaded, shelving a row of books at a time, and it helped me immensely. Those students inspired me to broaden the scope of this book to include children and elementary student volunteers. They helped me realize that people do not need to be adults with days off to donate time and help out.

All of these various positions, both as volunteer and employee, have helped me craft this book in a way that provides the bottom line of building a volunteer program, the background information needed to get it started, and innovative ideas to hook volunteers and keep them interested in the program. Once volunteers are invested, they will bring ideas to the table and help keep the program running smoothly, even expanding it beyond the organization's initial scope.

Chapter 1 defines volunteers, interns, and different classifications within those two broad terms. It explains how volunteers can help the library, and how they will learn their job duties without putting more responsibility on current library staff.

Chapter 2 delves into creating the program, deciding who will oversee the program, and how staff can help. Getting everyone on board will lighten the load of the volunteer coordinator or employee overseeing the program, as well as make volunteers feel like they are becoming part of a unified team.

Chapter 3 explains how to assess the library's needs in terms of what jobs need to be done, how many volunteers can be accommodated, and when they should work, in consideration of staff schedules and other events happening at the library. This chapter also explains writing job duty descriptions and special projects the library might want to propose to entice group or one-time volunteers.

Chapter 4 will help launch the volunteer program. Information about applications and tips about what should be included are in this chapter, as well as ideas for handling interviews with volunteers of different ages. This chapter lays the groundwork for information that may need to be included in the volunteer handbook and gives ideas about the most effective ways to train volunteers.

Chapter 5 dives into the different age groups of volunteers: adult, teen, and children. Information is broken down within each age group: "Job Duties," "Orientation," "Scheduling," "Checking In," and "Expanding the Job." Teen and children volunteer sections are further broken down into summer and school year volunteers for the public library, and student volunteers for school libraries.

Chapter 6 is all about growing and expanding the program. The value of volunteers section includes an in-depth interview with Dr. Sarah Petschonek, founder of Volunteer Odyssey, a volunteer hub in Memphis, Tennessee, that started as a way for job seekers to learn about local organizations while utilizing their skills. Chapter 6 includes information about spreading the word about the volunteer program, which naturally leads to library outreach. Outreach is more than making the library visible in the community—it is letting the community lead the library and curate it to fit the needs of the residents. Outreach organically increases library volunteers, and volunteers can help the library shift to be community-led, so it is all easier than it may seem on the surface. Becoming a community-led institution and outreach will help the library offer outside opportunities to volunteers and patrons, increasing the visibility of the library and all organizations that partner together.

Chapter 7 has examples of sample paperwork that can be copied and used to launch a volunteer program or can be slightly adapted and customized for specific library needs. Paperwork includes volunteer applications, the volunteer handbook, job description examples, and promotional material ideas and templates.

Library Volunteers: A Practical Guide for Librarians will help you create a volunteer program from the ground up, starting with the brainstorming phase. It will also open your mind to how people of different ages from different backgrounds can help out in so many different ways. You might think only adults can shelve books in alphabetical order, and teens can only help behind the scenes, but once you start exploring what needs to be done at your library, you will see how volunteers can benefit you in the smallest of ways. This will help your library grow in scope of services and programs offered, as well as allow your library to purposefully reach beyond its walls to influence the community.

About Volunteers

What is a Volunteer?

A VOLUNTEER IS A PERSON who performs a task for an organization without compensation. They are not employees of the organization but are committed to the organization's goals and help accomplish these goals by completing supplementary tasks. Volunteers are commonly adults, but as more middle and high schools require service hours, teens are becoming a sizable portion of the volunteer population. With libraries being pillars of their communities, it also makes sense that children be able to volunteer, if opportunities can be created. This book will cover the creation and implementation of a volunteer program that can support adult, teen, and children volunteers.

A long-term volunteer is someone who commits to the organization and feels strongly about the goals and mission of the group.[1] They often see themselves as leaders in the organization because of their devotion. They are invested and feel a sense of worth due to their work with the organization. Long-term volunteers may come to the organization because they already frequent the library, they want to explore the library's mission from inside the organization, or they know someone involved with the library and want to become a part of it themselves. Long-term volunteers may start with simple tasks that help employees, but usually feel empowered enough to create their own jobs and help in innovative ways. These volunteers may help start a volunteer program or come in soon after it is created, but they take pride in the organization and the volunteer help it provides and should be acknowledged for their dedication.

Short-term volunteers are interested in the organization and committed to its mission but might not be as strongly devoted as the long-term volunteers. They will do specific jobs to help the library but might not have the time or dedication to create their own job positions. They typically prefer to be fit into the program instead of structuring their own position within it. They might only volunteer for a few months to a year, on a semi-regular schedule, or they might prefer to help out with special events the library is organizing. These volunteers still feel fulfilled by their service, but they do not need to dedicate a lot of time and energy to it; they feel valued just by coming in and doing what is expected of them.

Within these two broad classifications of volunteers, there are many further break-downs, like retirees, students, professional volunteers, and transitional volunteers. Retirees no longer work full-time jobs, but still want to get out of the house and be involved in a way that gives back to the community. They might have more flexible schedules since they are not juggling a full-time job on top of other commitments, but they should not have to carry the volunteer program on their shoulders. Retirees can still have a lot going on in their lives, with appointments, family, free time, hobbies, and more, so they should not be called on any time the organization needs a set of helping hands—unless the volunteer explicitly asks to be called on with short notice!

Students can be high school students or college students. If the organization allows children to volunteer within certain limitations, then they might even be elementary school students. Though these volunteers are young, they can be very dedicated to the organization and might have great ideas on how to help the library evolve. These students are hopefully active users of the library, so going from being a library patron to a library volunteer and seeing how things work from the inside might light a spark within them.

Professional volunteers, or workplace volunteers, are often groups from a business or corporation who periodically devote an entire day of service to an organization. They might volunteer at the library quarterly, or twice a year, or just an annual day of service, but they are still a great source of volunteer time and involvement. An added bonus is that larger organizations often promote their service days, so the library will be associated with this day and get a lot of positive attention as a result. Some professional volunteers may come in independently to earn hours, for their job, as some organizations now request, or for their own personal satisfaction.

Transitional volunteers are a great untapped resource for service hours. Transitional volunteers are people who are out of work for a variety of reasons; maybe their company downsized, maybe they are looking for a new field, maybe they want to try different jobs before making a choice. These volunteers might have more flexibility, schedule-wise, and be more willing to try every job the library has to offer. If transitional volunteers know that they can get a reference letter from the library or the volunteer coordinator, there is no limit to the ideas and dedication they might bring on board. Advertising the volunteer program to people in transition is a great way to offer something different and make it easy for this population to try something new and get professional experience doing so.

Both long-term and short-term volunteers can greatly impact an agency. Long-term volunteers are ideal because they are so devoted to the organization they will inspire a lot of positive change and innovation. They also help keep the organization's mission on track by cutting down on volunteer turnover. Short-term volunteers, however, are great at helping the library get fresh ideas in from the public. They are often willing and flexible when it comes to when they can volunteer or what duties they can help with. Identifying volunteers as long-term or short-term should not affect the organization's relationship with them in any way, as all volunteers are valuable, however it is nice for the library to be able to define volunteers when assessing their own volunteer program needs.

An intern is a student enrolled in a higher learning program, or recently graduated from a higher learning platform, who commits to an organization for one semester or more. Interns may be compensated financially or with school credit through their institution. They might be looking for a position within the organization after they graduate, so they are a good source of volunteer time. Interns who want to succeed in the field will often have fresh, innovative ideas due to still be immersed in the academic world. They may have ideas for programs they would like to present and be able to conduct these programs for school project credit. This can greatly benefit the library by bringing in new programming and having a built-in programming lead to run it while other employees are busy. Depending on intern requirements for specific cities, states, schools, and organizations, interns may require different paperwork and procedures than volunteers. Information and resources in this book can easily be adapted to fit an internship program if there is a need in your community.

Volunteers and interns are resources that organizations need to utilize. Volunteers are often overlooked for various reasons, such as: creating a volunteer program is too much work, volunteers are not committed to the cause or the organization, there could be a high turnover in volunteers that costs the organization time and money, and more. The bottom line is that volunteers can greatly help any organization. They bring in different skills and have different backgrounds than people who are employed by the organization. Volunteers are not only extra sets of hands to help, but also extra sets of eyes that can give organizations fresh ideas for layout, services, promotion, and word of mouth. Volunteers are especially important to libraries, since libraries are often community centers and offer a variety of services to many different people. It only makes sense that the community come in to the library to help give back.

⑥ How Can Volunteers Help?

Volunteers are people who donate their time to organizations without expecting pay, but it is important that volunteers get something in return. This can be a chance to develop new job skills, credit for service hours, or a feeling of accomplishment for giving back. Potential volunteers should be evaluated during the application process to make sure the library will benefit from their help. Volunteers should value the library and all it offers and should want to help the library reach a broader scope in the community. They are a great way to spread the word about the library's services and programs because they are involved in the inner workings of the organization by choice. A good volunteer experience can ensure that positive word of mouth about your library will be shared with the community.

Both volunteers and the library should benefit from volunteering. The library will benefit from extra helping hands without overextending the budget. Volunteers are an ideal solution in the library environment, because library employees are often overworked and there is rarely room in the budget to pay for overtime or hire even part-time help. Duties like shelving, cleaning and repairing books, and maintaining shelves can fall to the wayside while employees focus on helping patrons, planning programs, and doing community outreach. Library maintenance tasks seem minor and are easily overlooked but are vital to running the library and having an attractive, navigable environment for patrons. Volunteers can pick up the slack by completing background duties while library employees focus on bigger picture job duties. Volunteers should not be depended on to complete duties integral to running the library.

Volunteer time was valued at just over $24 an hour in 2016, which is often much higher than library employees are paid for their work. "Nonprofits typically use the value of volunteer time to demonstrate the support they receive from their communities."[2] When putting a monetary value on volunteer hours, it makes it more obvious to organizations that it is worth investing time at the front end to creating a volunteer program. The amount of money saved in the long run by volunteers giving their time is paid off not only in the donated hours but also doubled by the work they complete in that time, as well as the work paid employees are freed up to complete.

For the sake of simplicity, the broad term "libraries" will refer to public libraries until specific sections on school and academic libraries. The paperwork provided at the end of this book is aimed at libraries but is general enough that it can be easily adapted for other organizations. The overall volunteer program structure and guidelines in this book can be slightly modified and applied to any organization that relies on and wants to encourage volunteer contributions.

Starting and maintaining a volunteer program in the library requires a lot of work on the front end but will pay off once volunteers are integrated into the library's daily duties. There are many jobs that need to be done for a library to run smoothly. Regarded as important public institutions and now seen more as community centers, libraries are often run on a very tight budget, and are understaffed with overworked employees. With people placing more value on libraries, many express interest in volunteering, but this often creates more work for library staff. Yes, library staff need help, but what can be handed over to a volunteer and completed satisfactorily? How can volunteers be recruited and trained and evaluated to ensure the library is benefitting from the additional hands on deck?

Building a program from scratch is the easiest way to make sure volunteers will benefit the library but adapting or modifying a current program is not at all difficult. Either way, it is important to remember to check in with your human resources and legal departments for guidelines. Stephen Ashley, a librarian in North Carolina, has worked as a volunteer coordinator in a variety of libraries. He notes that, while volunteer programs were already in place in each of his jobs, it was still a lot of work to coordinate the volunteers and their duties. "However, in at least one job, my position was new, so I was able to ease the burden on other staff by taking on volunteer coordination,"[3] Ashley adds. Having a specific volunteer coordinator is the best way to ensure the program runs smoothly and is least disruptive to other positions, but the entire library staff can, and will have to, work together to get the volunteer program up and running.

Ashley also mentions three main attributes that he sees as vital for a volunteer program to thrive:

1. Clear expectations, tasks, and guidelines—it should always be clear to volunteers what they should be doing and how they should be doing it.
2. Flexibility—being open about the types of tasks volunteers do can lead to more fulfilled volunteers who are more helpful to the library in general.
3. Staff support and buy-in—if staff are able to help and are just as welcoming to volunteers as the volunteer coordinator is, then the more efficiently the program can run.[4]

These major attributes will come up again and again in this guidebook because they are important to remember. Clarity, flexibility, and support will influence the library itself, the volunteers, the staff, and the actual volunteer program.

⑥ How Will They Learn?

When considering how volunteers will learn their job duties, it is important to also consider what they need to know. This can start on the application form, by asking what volunteers hope to get out of the experience. Remember that volunteers are donating their time for free, but hoping to be reimbursed in other ways, through learning new skills, being part of a team, helping a community organization grow, and more.

High school students might just need service hours and not care much about how they get the hours. Having them help prepare supplies and rooms for programs or shelving books might be a decent way for them to pass time while ensuring the library's duties are being satisfactorily completed. These tasks need to be done and will greatly impact the library, but they are not too time-consuming or difficult to learn for younger volunteers. They also require less oversight from a volunteer coordinator, freeing them up to focus on other aspects of the volunteer program. Guidelines can be set up so teens can simply come in, complete their tasks, and earn their hours while helping the library.

Some volunteers might just want to get out of the house and be involved in the community, so shelving books in the stacks where they can feel vital to the library's mission might be a good fit. Other volunteers might be considering a career change and would like to help with more involved library duties to prepare for their future library job. All of these purposes are valid, and all of these volunteers can help. But knowing the motivation behind your volunteers will help make sure both the library and the volunteer benefit from the commitment. It will also help the volunteer coordinator decide how their time is best spent; for example, is it more important to bring in a lot of volunteers to earn service hours, or to develop a more thorough training program that will rope in long-term volunteers who will help the library grow and change?

Volunteers are most likely people who frequent the library and want to help, but that does not mean they will know exactly what to do. Never assume that anyone has prior knowledge about how the library works; it is best to start from scratch with guidelines about the library, including physical layout, sections, shelving rules, where volunteers can be, how they should interact with the public, and more. Much of this information will be covered in your volunteer handbook but should also be covered in person so they can ask clarifying questions if necessary.

The first day of a new job can be nerve-wracking. Worrying about what to expect, how to act, where to go, and more makes it hard to remember the important instructions and tasks. When bringing in new volunteers, it is best to try and skip that feeling completely. People might still be nervous before starting something new, but the library needs to make sure volunteers are as prepared as possible to start their new positions. Holding volunteer orientations can greatly help prepare your volunteers. Give a tour of the library, explain how it is arranged and why. Show volunteers where they can take breaks, where they can use the restroom, and where to go to get a new task after they finish their first. Give them time to ask questions throughout the tour so they feel comfortable asking employees for help. Showing them the layout of the library and explaining how they fit in to the system gives the volunteers a solid background to start with. On their first day, they will feel familiar with the environment and will be able to get to work quickly. The orientation should also cut down on time spent asking questions the first day; frequent questions like, "Where is the bathroom?" or "What do I do now?" have already been answered during orientation.

While constructing the volunteer program and volunteer job descriptions, employees will write down their job duties that they would like volunteers to handle. Employees will also write down information about the volunteer tasks as if they were training someone new. Having each worker write a job description and steps for how to complete it will help jump-start the program because the library will already have jobs available for volunteers, as well as having an idea on how much time these tasks may take, and how they should be done. The information employees write about their jobs can be later used in the volunteer handbook's section on job descriptions.

Thinking about how volunteers will learn will naturally lead to thinking of how they will be evaluated. Employee evaluation forms and interviews are a good jumping off point for evaluations, but volunteers most likely will not need to be evaluated this thoroughly. A stripped-down version of standard evaluations would be a good baseline for volunteer evaluations but reading employees' self-described job descriptions would also be a logical starting point to build a custom volunteer evaluation form.

It is important to evaluate volunteers more often than you would evaluate employees because volunteer time commitments might have shorter spans. Evaluating often will also help volunteers feel supported; having job feedback and appreciation and being willing to help them do the task efficiently and correctly will make them want to work harder for you and stick around longer. Every evaluation does not have to be documented; an evaluation can be an informal check-in while your volunteer is preparing program supplies or shelving books. The volunteer coordinator making their presence known and being visible and accessible will help volunteers feel comfortable with their task and with asking questions.

Volunteers who have committed to a long term, or who have or will stay for a long time, might enjoy a "promotion." This does not mean they will be hired for a full-time position, but rewards are welcomed, especially when people are donating their time for free. Will there be some sort of hierarchy for volunteers, or perks when it comes to picking new tasks or shifts? Will senior volunteers be able to train newcomers? This would not only make dedicated volunteers feel a sense of accomplishment, but it would help the volunteer coordinator as well. While they are helping the library grow and evolve, volunteers should feel like they are growing and evolving in their positions. They should be rewarded with positive feedback, a chance to share input about library programs and services, and more responsibility.

Key Points

- A volunteer is a person who performs a task for an organization without compensation.
- Volunteers are commonly adults, but with schools requiring service hours, teens are becoming a sizable portion of the volunteer population.
- Though volunteers are not paid, volunteers should still get something from their volunteer commitment, such as learning new skills or being part of a team.

- Volunteers can help with tasks typically done around the library, or custom tasks can be created for volunteer projects.
- Volunteers should be evaluated like employees are, so they can share their feedback, suggest changes, and feel valued as part of the team.

Notes

1. McCurley, Stephen, and Rick Lynch. *Volunteer Management: Mobilizing All the Resources in the Community*. Downers Grove, IL: Heritage Arts Publishing, 1996.
2. "What Is the Monetary Value of Volunteer Time?" GrantSpace. Accessed August 1, 2019. http://www.grantspace.org/resources/knowledge-base/monetary-value-of-volunteer-time/.
3. "Interview with Stephen Ashley." Email interview by author. July 16, 2018.
4. "Interview with Stephen Ashley." Email interview by author. July 16, 2018.

References

"Interview with Stephen Ashley." Email interview by author. July 16, 2018.

McCurley, Stephen, and Rick Lynch. *Volunteer Management: Mobilizing All the Resources in the Community*. Downers Grove, IL: Heritage Arts Publishing, 1996.

"What Is the Monetary Value of Volunteer Time?" GrantSpace. Accessed August 1, 2019. http://www.grantspace.org/resources/knowledge-base/monetary-value-of-volunteer-time/.

Creating a Program

Creating a Volunteer Program

DECIDING TO CREATE a volunteer program is a big step for the library that will have major payoffs. Much of the background work will be available in this book, such as sample applications and handbooks, ideas for promotional materials, and guidelines for scheduling and evaluating volunteers, with the goal of expanding the program. It sounds like a daunting task, but it is relatively simple to get the framework built, and once volunteers are brought on board, the program will stand on its own and develop over time.

It is important, before creating a volunteer program, to know that you will be able to find volunteers. Think about the library's patrons and the community the library serves; will any of these people be willing volunteers? Are there colleges or high schools nearby? Scout groups or other youth organizations that need service projects and service hours? It would be beneficial to conduct a survey of the community, even an informal one. Ask patrons if they would be interested in volunteering, or know anyone who would be, as they stop by the reference desk or check out books. Contact professors at nearby colleges to see if any students need school credit or internship hours from the library. Reach out to the guidance counselors and club leaders at nearby high schools to see if students need service hours for honors societies or other clubs. Mention that volunteering at the library can be a good work experience for teens, and that they will get a letter of recommendation for future volunteer or job opportunities, as well as for college applications. Putting the possibility of a volunteer program out to the community might bring potential volunteers out of the woodwork. Make it clear that the program will be established with scheduling possibilities, set job descriptions, and perks. Patrons might be interested, even though they never thought to offer their time to the library. Knowing it is an opportunity that will be offered to them might make it seem more plausible, instead of having to do the legwork of asking for an opportunity, making a schedule, and figuring out a task for themselves.

After assessing who might be a potential volunteer, the library's needs should be assessed. This will be further explored in chapter 3, but includes thinking of jobs for volunteers to do, and when they need to be done. Shelving might need to be done the last two hours before closing, to free up staff to do other duties. Or evenings might be too busy, with too many patrons trying to conduct research and use computers and check out last-minute books before the doors are locked, so there might not be room for volunteers at that time. Map out what will work best for the library as it is now; is the children's section too busy during the mornings due to storytimes and parents visiting with their toddlers? Do not schedule any volunteer tasks for that area. If shelvers are scheduled to work in a section that is already busy, patrons might be agitated at the inconvenience of another person and a book cart in their way, and volunteers might get frustrated that they are unable to do their assigned task. Planning around issues like these on the front end will ensure the volunteer program runs smoothly from the start, instead of causing troubles that need to be solved when volunteers are already on board. Get as much figured out on the front end as possible! There will be plenty of other hiccups down the road that are impossible to see coming until actual volunteers are in place.

After the library's needs are listed, consider how a volunteer could solve these problems. If there is rarely an employee to shelve books, then at least one volunteer job should be shelving. If there are many sections of shelving that get backed up, give each section its own job description and subsequent volunteer. Some libraries might have needs that relate to outreach, social media, and promotion. These can be addressed with volunteers, but it is important to tread carefully. The library needs to always appear professional and welcoming when it comes to its public face, and a volunteer might not understand the library's values. Giving a volunteer access to the library's social media channels might not be the best option but allowing volunteers to pitch ideas for social media posts and captions could work. They could submit pictures of their duties and write a brief statement about what they are doing and how it makes them feel. This way, volunteers can still help the library by creating content to share publicly, but the images and text will go through a library employee before it is seen by the world. This counts as volunteer time and also still helps cut down on library employees' workloads, so it might be an ideal solution to the library's social media need. There are creative ways to utilize and empower employees while still greatly benefitting the library and cutting down on the tasks put upon library employees' shoulders. Look at each of the library's needs with a critical and creative eye and see how volunteers can be used.

Library volunteers can fit into the overall structure of the library in a variety of ways. Volunteers can fit in like puzzle pieces, filling gaps left by employees because they are too busy with other tasks.[1] This method obviously helps the library because volunteers can fill in to do these jobs that are otherwise left incomplete because employees are busy with more pressing tasks. This means the library will be able to have a broader scope of services and programs to offer the public since volunteers are helping more within the library with other tasks. Volunteers helping in a library can also look more like a Venn diagram, with library staff duties overlapping with volunteer duties. This means that volunteers are helping take some stress off of library employees because they are doing the same jobs that are assigned to staff. Either way volunteers fit into the library will benefit all involved.

⊚ Who Will Run the Program?

Ideally, a volunteer coordinator will run the volunteer program. If the library branch or overall system can hire a volunteer coordinator, it will make developing and implementing the program run very smoothly, and start benefiting the library immediately. However, libraries are already working with limited budgets, so hiring an additional employee, especially one with such specific duties, might not be plausible. If such expenses can be brought before the board, the Friends group, library administration, or even city or county government, it is worth a try. Volunteers will bring so much to the libraries that they will end up saving the library a lot of money, while helping it expand its capacities. This means that the salary of the volunteer coordinator will easily be earned back by donated hours from volunteers, and then some!

If there is not an individual who can devote their work hours to the volunteer program, then it is possible to build and start the program slower, and on a smaller scale, so it will not tax any of the current library employees. While different ages can volunteer, it might be ideal to have a librarian working in adult services dedicate more time to the program initially, and work as an acting volunteer coordinator. This is because adults will most likely be the first volunteers to come on board, the easiest to train and bring in, and will require less oversight quickly. Also, once adult volunteers are trained and found to be doing great work, they could be "promoted" to help oversee and even run the program from the inside, making it a true volunteer program. This means that, with just a little work on the front end, the library employee who acts as the volunteer coordinator will not have to shoulder that load for long.

On the other hand, using a teen services librarian could be beneficial if the plan is to launch the volunteer program for summer. Summer means teens will be out of school, looking for things to do and ways to earn service hours. Building the program in the spring will help the library be ready to hire teen volunteers for the summer, and they will be able to help greatly with summer library duties in addition to whatever summer learning programs the library will offer. Once summer is over, the teen services librarian can apply the experience toward creating a year-round volunteer program for all ages. The knowledge from the summer volunteers will help a lot with planning for best and worst case scenarios, as summers are usually a busy and unpredictable time even without volunteers thrown into the mix! Using this method, the volunteer program could easily be developed over the calendar year, with a goal of having volunteers help train incoming volunteers by the next fall, which would lighten the teen services librarian's volunteer coordinator duties.

There is nothing wrong with trying to create a more unstructured volunteer program that will be volunteer-run, as in the style of a neighborhood watch program. If the library has an enthusiastic patron or someone who has already started volunteering, they might be willing to oversee the program. If a volunteer is willing to be a leader within the program, then library staff and management can help create the backbone of the program and know they are leaving it in capable hands. This lead volunteer can be involved in creating the program; if they are interested in or already volunteering with the library, they will have good input. This volunteer does not have to remain the leader of the program for its entire run; they can train another volunteer to help run it, or once more volunteers are recruited, it can be more of an independently run program where everyone is responsible for themselves. The good thing is, once the background paperwork has been created and volunteers are introduced to it, it will be no problem for them to govern themselves. After an interview, orientation, and brief training, volunteers can write in shifts on a volunteer schedule so the library employees are aware of when they will have help, they can pick their own job duties, and keep track of their own hours.

Implementing a volunteer-run program does not mean that the program will be any less effective, and it does not mean the library is cutting corners when it comes to their volunteers. In fact, a lot of volunteers would prefer to be self-governed since they are already taking a large initiative by donating their time and skills to the organization. It is also a reasonable goal for the library to start with a more structured program and aim toward having a volunteer-run program a few years down the line.

SRVS, Memphis-area organization that provides a variety of services for people with disabilities and their families, started a volunteer program from a volunteer. The volunteer came on a tour of the organization, fell in love with its mission, and wanted to help in any way possible. After assisting in weekly art classes for a few months, SRVS decided they wanted to start a full-scale volunteer program. The original volunteer worked with the Learning Center management and public relations team to develop a volunteer application and handbook. The screening process took some work, since volunteers would be working directly with people with disabilities. The background checks and liability forms required for this organization do not directly apply to library volunteers, so they have been excluded from this manual, but might be required depending on government jurisdiction and what population volunteers will be working with. Despite the added "hurdles" of background checks, liability forms, and online training courses about Health Insurance Portability and Accountability Act (HIPAA) and Department of Intellectual and Developmental Disabilities (DIDD), the organization quickly built an effective volunteer program. Do not think that any volunteer requirements or job duties are too much to ask of a volunteer! If someone is passionate, they will want to help the organization, and these are the volunteers the library wants on their side.

Overall, it depends on the library's patronage, hours, and staff. Who is most interested in working with volunteers? Who would benefit from it most? Who has a little time in their schedule, or can be more flexible with their hours? Keep in mind that starting a volunteer program does not need to be a major point of stress. Volunteers exist to help lighten the load of organizations that employ them. A volunteer program can be planned and launched in a couple of months, or it can be developed slowly over a year and implemented at the beginning of the next calendar year. There is no right or wrong way to develop the volunteer program, but if it is too stressful on an organization and its employees, then it is best to take a step back, reevaluate what the organization needs, and reassess how it is approaching this solution.

It is the goal of this handbook to do the majority of the background work of starting a volunteer program. By providing sample applications, handbooks, promotional materials, and ideas for job descriptions and scheduling, the employees who are tasked with creating the volunteer program will be freed up to do the legwork of recruiting and training volunteers in person.

Initially, bringing in volunteers might seem like more trouble than it is worth. More people will be in the library more consistently, and they might not seem to fit in with library staff or might seem like cogs in the well-oiled library machine.

It is usually best to have one contact person for volunteers, typically the volunteer coordinator, to keep everything consistent and easy to manage. It is also best that this one person be passionate about volunteering, because volunteer management is a lot of work. Make sure employees know that they will all have to interact and welcome volunteers in some way. In a staff meeting, ask who would want to take on this additional responsibility. If possible, shuffle some tasks around so the new volunteer coordinator is taking on this huge role without being piled on.

If the volunteer program is going to get larger over time, it might be best for a library employee who works in Adult Services handle the adult volunteers, and a library employee who works in Teen Services to handle teen volunteers. Since the library employees who deal with each age group will have more familiarity with that population, it will make sense for them to help customize the volunteer program for their groups.

Whether the library has one employee working as a volunteer coordinator, or one for each age group, it is important to decide how much time needs to be dedicated to the volunteer program. How often will potential new volunteers be interviewed? How often will the coordinator conduct new volunteer orientations? This is something best discussed in a staff meeting so everyone will be on board. It is important that all employees know the basics of how the program will run, so everyone can give information to library patrons and potential volunteers—correct information, and consistent information. It is also important that all employees know the additional work that will go into the program, so they can help with the volunteer coordinator's other tasks. Letting all workers see how the program should run will build a solid foundation for the library and will help the volunteers fit into the environment more seamlessly.

To get library staff on board, have meetings and regularly check in with employees to see how they feel and what they are thinking about the program. What are they worried about? What tasks would they like to delegate to a volunteer? Would they prefer to be more hands on or hands off with the volunteers?

Keep the floor open. Let workers voice their concerns about the volunteer program and what additional work it might create. Make sure staff feel heard, and always take their input into consideration. If regular staff meetings are held during the volunteer program planning, then there will be a good base for employee input.

It is not uncommon for staff to feel slightly resentful of new people coming in to their space and trying to do their jobs—especially if volunteers are viewed as doing it for "fun" and for free. But instead of feeling threatened by the volunteers, make sure staff sees them as helpers, people coming to make their jobs easier. Do not let staff feel put out by volunteers' questions—it is expected to have questions as volunteers take on new tasks, and it is better for volunteers to ask first instead of doing a task incorrectly. Having a set volunteer coordinator or coordinators will come in handy, because questions can be directed to one person. However, everyone should be team players, working toward the same goal while trying to make that goal easier to reach. That is another reason why it is so important for everyone to have the same information about the volunteer program. It is inconsistent to have one employee saying a certain thing about a task while the volunteer coordinator has a different answer to the same question.

Stephen Ashley has worked as a volunteer coordinator for a variety of libraries, and notes that staff buy-in is incredibly important to allow a volunteer program to run smoothly.

> Flexibility, kindness, and understanding are very important. It's important to remember that volunteers are helping without any financial compensation. While they may get some personal benefits from volunteering, it's important to remember they are there because they want to be, in general. If an organization can be accommodating to the needs of volunteers and show appreciation for their volunteers, then that is a good place to volunteer. Libraries should welcome volunteers in the same way they welcome their patrons.
>
> It's also good when an organization has a clear plan for volunteers with guidelines and expectations. Volunteers may not have a deep enough understanding of the organization to know exactly what they should be doing at all times, so it's best when it's always clear what they should be doing and how they should be doing it.[2]

It is important to remember that it is impossible to make everyone happy. Once the volunteer program is in place, staff might become more satisfied as they see results. Seeing how the volunteer program works might also make some employees want to help out more. They might be more willing to train volunteers or delegate more tasks when they see that the quality of work will not suffer just because someone is doing it for free.

Something to include in volunteer evaluation forms might be a section for feedback from staff and, if applicable, patrons. Does one volunteer have a few complaints that they have not done the job correctly, or do not stay on task while they are on the clock? Do they ask library workers too many questions that make their time as a volunteer more of a hindrance than a help? Do they talk too much to patrons? Keeping staff on board with the volunteer program can really depend on how the volunteers are treated in relation to staff. Everyone should be treated equally, though volunteers are giving their time for free, so sometimes it might seem necessary to appease them more than paid workers. But if a volunteer is not doing a good job or is making an employee feel stressed or uneasy, it is not worth ignoring an employee's feelings just to get free help for the library.

Checking in with staff should not end once the volunteer program is implemented. Keep checking in to get feedback, ideas for new tasks or ways to refine the workflow, and to make sure staff feels valued and comfortable.

⊚ Key Points

- Think of where the library can find volunteers from the community and start laying the groundwork on establishing the program.
- Make a list of library tasks and brainstorm how volunteers can help complete these jobs.
- Ideally, a volunteer coordinator will run the program and help manage the volunteers. If this position cannot be created, the volunteer coordinator duties can be spread across a couple of employees in various ways.

- It is also possible for a volunteer program to be entirely volunteer-led. This will initially take some work but can pay off in the long run.
- Get staff on board with the volunteer program start-up and keep them involved in the planning and implementation. They will be the volunteer program's strongest allies.
- Volunteers need management just as much as employees do. They need check ins and guidance about the quality of their work.
- Volunteers are donating their time to the library. Make sure they have meaningful tasks to keep them occupied during their entire shift.

Notes

1. McCurley, Stephen, and Rick Lynch. *Volunteer Management: Mobilizing All the Resources in the Community*. Downers Grove, IL: Heritage Arts Publishing, 1996.
2. "Interview with Stephen Ashley." Email interview by author. July 16, 2018.

References

"Interview with Stephen Ashley." Email interview by author. July 16, 2018.
McCurley, Stephen, and Rick Lynch. *Volunteer Management: Mobilizing All the Resources in the Community*. Downers Grove, IL: Heritage Arts Publishing, 1996.

Assessing Library Needs

Assessing Library Needs

HAVE EMPLOYEES MAKE LISTS of all the library-related tasks they do, and additional projects they would like to take on if they had the time and resources. These projects can be far-fetched—the point is to get all the ideas out and flowing. Make a list of goals for the library, like to have a more established social media presence, to have volunteer applications and handbooks accessible on the website, do more outreach beyond the library walls, and so on. Even if a task does not initially seem suitable for a volunteer, write it down because there might be ways to break it down and turn it into something a volunteer can easily help with.

Once the task list is complete, look at it with a critical eye. These lists will come into play later, when considering what jobs need to be done and how to write job duty descriptions, so they will get fleshed out in the process. It will be obvious to see how volunteers can help with certain tasks, like shelving or cleaning up after programs. Some might be harder to assign to volunteers due to liability or privacy level of the task. Volunteers should not, for example, have access to patrons' records. Volunteers should not be left alone with children in a program room unless they have completed a background check as required by the library administration. Volunteers should not be able to publicly represent the library as the library itself, such as at public events or through the library's online outlets. Remember, though, they are more than able to share their personal experiences with the library and its volunteer program however they see fit, so make sure their library experiences are positive ones that will help the library increase in patrons, program attendance, and volunteers.

Even if tasks are not obviously suited for volunteers, it is possible to make it work. Some volunteers might have an information technology background that could make them useful for simple library technology problems. If the library's computer is acting up, can they fix it while an employee helps a patron instead? Can the volunteer clear a printer jam? Can the volunteer help patrons working on computers who have technical questions? Be careful that the last option of technology help does not infringe on the patron's privacy or make the volunteer uncomfortable. The goal of the program is to benefit the library, yes, but it is also vital that the volunteers feel safe and appreciated. Helping with technological questions might be a blurry line that needs to be inspected by library management and administration, but so many questions relate to the library's computers that it would really free up employees if volunteers could take on this task.

What special projects can the library realistically try to take on over the next year? If time can be helped with volunteers but the financial resources or physical materials are not available, that project can go on the back burner until a later time. Having a major project goal for the library to accomplish, utilizing volunteers, within the first year of a volunteer program is a good way to show the board, Friends groups, administration, and the city and county governments how effective volunteer help actually is for the library. This can help the volunteer program get more financial assistance and even convince those in charge that a volunteer coordinator needs to be hired to manage the program, if this was initially an expense that was rejected.

How many volunteers could the library use? Would a handful of regular volunteers be better than groups coming to volunteer for an entire day? Are there projects and duties to accommodate various volunteers' skill sets and schedules?

Consider library's size and layout. Consider how many employees are working at certain times. Consider lunch breaks and other breaks employees and volunteers might take. Take the list of job duties and assess where the tasks will take place and how long it will take to complete them. These factors determine how many volunteers the library can handle at different times.

Look at employees' task breakdowns and think about how long each task will take. Think about how many people need to do each task—is it solitary, like shelving, or a group task, like shifting shelves? How often do these tasks need to be done? Shelving is an ongoing job, so it might be no problem to have enough for a two-hour shift every Monday afternoon. Is there enough work for a different volunteer to do the same on Tuesday? Wednesday? Write these down to start a schedule, which will help figure out how many people are needed. Also consider what age group could do these tasks—make sure the library can offer meaningful tasks to volunteers of all ages.

Assessing volunteer tasks in relation to time in this manner will help with scheduling volunteers, whether they want to sign up for regular tasks, or are coming in as they have time. Always try to have another task or two as backup—it is better to have jobs that do not get completed than to have a volunteer work for an hour, then sit around for an hour. They are donating their time to help, so they need to feel useful. This will affect their word of mouth about the library and volunteer program. Volunteers who work and help the library will feel fulfilled and spread the word about how productive it makes them feel.

It might be easiest to limit volunteers as the program is first launched. Once a list of tasks is completed, decide if the library needs to start with two adults and two teens, or four adults and no teens. As the application pool grows, hire quality volunteers who seem most likely to help the library reach its goals. It may be best to hire volunteers at the speed the library needs them, but program launch deadlines can help. If volunteers need to be contributing a certain amount of time to the library's bottom line three months after the program launch, this needs to be factored into the hiring process.

Volunteers might have more flexible schedules and can fill in the blanks when the library is understaffed, when people take lunch breaks, when an employee is busy in a program, and more. Having a lot of volunteers does not mean they have to all work at the same time, so the library does not need to be overrun with volunteers.

If the program grows exponentially and seems too large, it is possible to pare down volunteers or work on scheduling them more efficiently. If troubleshooting does not work, it is acceptable to let volunteers go. Managing and evaluating volunteers periodically can help with this potential problem. The number of volunteers and hours they put in will affect how much work the volunteer coordinator will put in on the management side. The coordinator will have to log the hours, keep track of signing in and out, and make sure the volunteers have plenty to do. The more volunteers hired, the more work the volunteer coordinator will have—at least on the front end, until the program is established and will run more smoothly.

⑨ What Jobs Need to be Done

Are library workers doing tasks that volunteers could easily do? Is there a reason that a library worker needs to do a specific task? There is, of course, a major difference between a volunteer cutting out supplies for a storytime craft compared to taking pictures to post on the library's official social media outlets. Even if volunteers are professional adults, always be aware of what the library is showing the public. Make sure volunteers get enjoyable tasks, though; do not just dump the mundane work on them, or they will not want to give their time. Official public outreach might not be a volunteer duty, but word of mouth is always helpful. Make sure volunteers are satisfied in their positions and will speak highly of the library to the public.

Have a staff meeting to talk about the library's volunteer program. Ask library workers to make a list of their job duties. Look at those duties in different ways:

- Rank them in order of importance to the employee.
- Rank them in order of importance to the library branch.
- Rank them in order of enjoyment by the employee.
- Is there is any overlap of what each employee does?

Share these lists and talk about what volunteers could do to make things easier on staff while helping the library. Do employees dislike shelving books? Do they have trouble escaping the desk to hang posters for their programs? Is there ever time to clean books, especially picture books?

Write down these tasks and assess if volunteers could do them: Can these tasks be completed in a short volunteer shift? Are the tasks better suited to individual volunteers, or for a larger group? Shelving is typically a great volunteer duty. Volunteers can be assigned a section or genre or even a letter, depending on the size of the library's collection and how many volunteers have signed up. Shelving is never done, of course, but a lot can be accomplished during a few volunteer hours. Cleaning books can be a good task for groups that come to the library to get service hours, because a whole section can be cleaned quickly while they work together.

Volunteers can easily help hang posters for programs on library bulletin boards and stand up displays. They can distribute stacks of take-home flyers to each station at the circulation desk. They can even deliver flyers and posters to local businesses, if they are willing to use their car to do volunteer errands. If the library has not reached out to local businesses to see if they can promote library events on the business's bulletin board, the volunteer might be able to help. Use volunteers' connections to the library's advantage; if the volunteer knows the manager of a nearby business, perhaps they could ask about hanging flyers on the library's behalf.

Once staff sees what jobs they are responsible for, they will more clearly see how volunteers can help. Most employees will probably want to start by getting rid of their least enjoyable jobs, which can be fine, as long as volunteers are allowed a little flexibility in how they approach the job and how often they do it. Volunteers might enjoy tasks that employees dislike because they are new to the library and have not gotten burned out on certain jobs, or because they have more time to give to help instead of feeling like they have to accomplish certain tasks.

Try to find out why employees dislike certain tasks. Is it because they do not often have time to shelve books? Is it because cleaning picture books is so time-consuming, they have to work on program planning or record keeping at home? Or is it because the cleanser used on picture book covers dries out their skin and smells awful? It is a good idea to find out a little more about why employees dislike tasks because these issues can be fixed—for both employees and volunteers! No one wants to dry their skin out and breathe an awful chemical for hours while they are donating their time. Can the library purchase a different cleanser? Would this make the employee want to take back their task, or are they still open to volunteer help?

Some employees might be overprotective of their job duties. They might like things done a certain way, and volunteers will do them differently. Or they might worry that the volunteers will outshine them. Reassure staff that volunteers are only here to help, not to replace anyone, and not to try and change the way tasks are done. Giving employees the power to write their own job descriptions and steps to complete a task will help them see that they can still have a bit of control over the situation. If the children's librarian likes books displayed in the children's section on the tops of every other shelf, that can be written into the job description and explained to the volunteer when the time comes. The librarian can also still pick the books to display and put them on a cart for the volunteer to put out. Having a volunteer to put up display books does not mean the volunteer can do whatever they want—everyone is still working toward the library's mission. Volunteers are helping hands coming in to make sure library staff can do everything they need and want to do.

Make it clear that volunteers are welcome to share feedback, though. Staff should not think they can boss volunteers around or treat them like they are not a part of the team.

Volunteers should be treated as well as employees and valued because they are willingly giving their time. It might be easy to dismiss any volunteer suggestions because they are not in the library full time, like most employees, but they are still valuable. Volunteers are coming into the library with diverse backgrounds and might have input on how the library is functioning and what could change. Every suggestion might not be implemented, but it is important that volunteers feel free to share ideas with no negative repercussions from staff.

⑥ Job Duty Descriptions

After evaluating what duties are staff duties and what can be done by volunteers, further break down tasks into what can be done by volunteers alone, and what might require some oversight. Shelving, for example, can be done completely by volunteers once they know how the library's shelving system works. That can be done with an initial training, so it will not require much oversight. Helping prepare for programs, however, might require some more oversight since volunteers will be working with supplies that might be limited, and if something gets prepared incorrectly, might affect the outcome of the program.

Employees have already done a lot of the legwork when it comes to writing up job duties for the volunteers. They wrote lists of their tasks and then broke it down into information about how to complete them, and what the finished job should look like. The job duties are basically completely written!

These descriptions will be included in a specific section of the volunteer handbook, so it is important to look them over carefully as employees turn them in. Edit them so they are easy to understand and keep the format of each duty the same so volunteers can easily pick different duties without needing much instruction or oversight.

- Each job should have a title.
- Each job should have a description.
- Each job should be broken down into manageable tasks that show volunteers how to complete them.
- Each job should end with a brief description about how the volunteer will know the job is completed. For example: the books are shelved alphabetically; all the magazines have been moved to the new section; the craft supplies are stacked up on the cart for storytime.

It might seem like overkill but having thorough descriptions will empower the volunteers—they can read the manual and know exactly what to do. It is also useful to post these descriptions near the volunteers' sign-in sheet or keep them in a binder there. This will help the volunteer coordinator because less questions will be coming in about what the jobs require—volunteers will be able to read over the descriptions on their own.

Also consider having simple jobs or breaking a larger job into smaller tasks that can be done by people with different abilities and different time constraints. An inclusive volunteer program is best because there will be no limits to who can come in to help, and when.

Allison Renner was a Teen Services Librarian and teen volunteer coordinator at a branch of the Memphis Public Libraries. When asked about inclusive tasks, Renner shared this story:

> One of my best groups of volunteers was a special education functional skills class that came once a month. They came from a high school far away from my library branch; the teachers tried to find volunteer opportunities at libraries closer to their school, but none would accept them. My library was more than willing to have eager volunteers on board, so we found tasks for them to do. The large group was broken into two, and two teachers stayed with each group. One group set up camp in the children's section and cleaned picture books. Another group would help shelve novels in the young adult section. When they were done, and the picture books were clean, this group would also help reshelve the children's books. Each group needed more oversight and guidance than usual volunteers, but the time and effort they put into the library was much appreciated. As a result, they felt invested in the library and proud of the work they did. This benefited the library through their work, of course, but also increased our statistics regarding volunteer hours, library visitors in and out, and the word of mouth from these students and teachers was invaluable. We were able to reach citizens in a different community and encourage them to visit our library over others.

Having small tasks also helps with time management for other volunteers. If a teen has half an hour to kill between school and their job, they could easily shelve a row of books in the young adult section. Small tasks help larger jobs get done, even if it is incrementally. Small portions of time still help volunteer hour statistics, and volunteers will feel valued because they are still welcomed to help even if they cannot guarantee a large chunk of time at once.

Always be open to job duties that might come up in the future, and dream big—if the library could have as many volunteers as it needed, to work on any project that needed to be completed, what would that look like? Think about upcoming holiday programs, theme months, special weeks, and, of course, summer. How could volunteers help the library go above and beyond in these aspects? A lot of holiday and summer programs will create one-time opportunities for volunteers. It might require more of the volunteers' time, but just for one day, like having people man stations for the summer learning kick-off party. Besides year-round volunteer opportunities, make sure to mention potential special projects in the volunteer handbook so people know they can still help with one-off projects even if they cannot commit to a regular schedule.

Think about seasonal projects as well. Does the library have plants or flowers on the lawn? This requires upkeep, and while the library system or city might fund it, volunteers might like to help. Some library patrons could be avid gardeners and having a chance to make their local library beautiful might inspire them to help. Word of mouth might spread to Master Gardeners or other related groups in the community, increasing the scope of the library and its volunteer program. Volunteers could also help employees man pop-up library booths at community events, farmers markets, or even the mall! Volunteers helping outside of the library building are still great volunteers—they are becoming invested in the library, and that is always a positive thing.

⊚ How Many Volunteers Are Needed?

Regardless of how many jobs the library has created and how much work needs to be done, it is important to start with a few volunteers, much fewer than the library would ideally like to hire. Starting with one volunteer is better than starting with ten, but if a small group of four volunteers, preferably of the same age group, can start at the same time, it would work well. This way the volunteer coordinator can lead a group orientation and training, but if volunteers also need individual training, the volunteer coordinator will not have a lot of extra work to take on. Four volunteers will also give the library a good idea of how volunteers can work in the library. Are they keeping their commitment? Are they showing up for shifts and completing the work in the allotted time? Four is also a good number because they will all have different experiences volunteering at the library, and the coordinator can check in with them regularly to see how things are going. These volunteers will have different feedback and input about the volunteer program, but the suggestions they give will not be overwhelming to implement. Starting with a few volunteers will also allow the volunteer coordinator to assess the program and make necessary changes without having to disrupt the schedule and workflow of a large number of volunteers.

Once the first few volunteers are brought on board and the program is assessed and tweaked, the volunteer coordinator can open an application period to hire more volunteers. This might mean hiring more volunteers in the same age group; for example, growing the program to ten adult volunteers when it initially started with four adults. Or the volunteer coordinator and library overall might feel ready to open up the program to teen and even children volunteers as well. Opening the program up to all ages will help it grow, so it might be best to stagger these application periods to keep the volunteer coordinator from getting overwhelmed with work, and to keep the library from getting overrun with volunteers. Having too many volunteers might sound like a good problem to have, but it can stress out the coordinator and the program as a whole. If the wait time to be interviewed and attend orientation is too long, volunteers might lose interest. If the schedule is booked with volunteers and potential help cannot find a time to volunteer, they might be discouraged and not come back. Therefore it is best to start each program slowly with soft launches of bringing in a few volunteers and getting them acclimated before deciding to bring on more.

When the program is launched, there might be a need for more volunteers, and applications can be accepted at any time instead of just during certain periods. The volunteer coordinator might find that the majority of volunteers only come in once a week, leaving gaps in the schedule that need to be filled. Or maybe most current volunteers can only come in on weekends, so applicants who can help during the week need to be hired. This can be stated on the library's website and social media, told to potential volunteers as they take an application, or just dealt with on the back end as volunteer applications come in. The volunteer coordinator can interview and hire those who say they are available when the library needs them.

Always remember to send polite emails to potential volunteers who do not fit in with the library and make it clear that they are appreciated and might be needed in time. It is a good idea to keep in touch with these potential volunteers and be kind and professional in all correspondence, so they will remain interested in helping the library. Just because someone is willing to donate their time to the library for free does not mean that they will be sitting around waiting for a position and jump at the chance whenever it is offered.

Their applications and contact information can be kept for when there is volunteer turnover or a need to bring on more volunteers, and it is better to have reached out to them prior than to never acknowledge their application until they are needed months later. These volunteers can also be contacted to help with special projects, group events, or one-off library programs when a bunch of help is needed in addition to the regular volunteers.

⑥ Special Projects

Ideally, the library will always have a special project or two on the back burner. Scout groups or other community organizations might request a day of service at the library, and instead of having to scramble to come up with enough books for a group of fifteen teens to shelve, it would be nice to have a project ready to go. If no community groups ever contact the library about days of service, then reach out to them. Scout groups and youth groups especially love taking on service projects because it fulfills requirements for their organization. Adult service groups will likely be willing to help because they can be more flexible with their commitment and the scope of their work. Some workplaces also participate in days of service or encourage their employees to volunteer. Reaching out to local businesses, even corporations, will only broaden the scope of your volunteer program. The worst case scenario is that the businesses are not interested in service hours, but now know about the library's volunteer program, so the time is still well spent by spreading the word.

One idea for a special project is to clean the children's books. These books get handled so frequently that they get dirty and sticky but are put back on the shelf before an employee can make time to wipe them off. Get enough cleaning supplies to accommodate a group—remember, they can share—and set them up in the appropriate section. A couple of volunteers can start at the beginning of the section, a couple in the middle, and a couple at the end. This ensures there is enough room for volunteers to take books from the shelf, clean them, wipe them off, and reshelve them. If there are more volunteers than can fit in one section, offer book carts to a few. They can load a shelf of books onto the cart, go to another area to clean the books, then bring them back to the shelves.

Another special project can be landscaping. A group of volunteers can help prune bushes and plants around the library, or plant new ones. If the library has planters on the grounds or at the entryway, volunteer groups can be scheduled seasonally to change out the plants and flowers growing in the planters. Volunteers can pick up any trash on the library grounds, rake up leaves, and sweep the entryway. This task will depend on weather and season, so you might need a fallback task so volunteers do not cancel the day of, or feel like they are giving their time to the library with no task to do.

Helping to move sections of books can be a good group volunteer task. Trying to make an independent section for graphic novels when they are currently shelved in the nonfiction one according to Dewey Decimal number is a huge undertaking. It involves a lot of shifting books and shelves, even if there is already a new section of shelving for graphic novels. If a group comes in, some volunteers can move and arrange graphic novels on the empty shelves while others shift the nonfiction books to cover the gap of empty shelves left by the move. This can also be used as a project when outdated materials are being weeded, like VHS or cassette tapes some libraries still have taking up shelf space.

Weeding is a good group task because entire sections can be done quickly. Like with cleaning books, station volunteers far enough apart where they have their own space and shelves to weed without stepping on each other. Print out lists of books that have not circulated for years, or that are marked lost or missing. Give volunteers empty book carts, just a couple per section to share, and have them pull all the books they can find. They can make a note about books that are not on the shelves and might actually be lost or missing, which will help the library update their records.

Another good group task is one that might not be as popular because it is not really hands-on work, but the volunteer coordinator can stress this job's importance to potential volunteers. Shelf reading is something that benefits the library so much, but rarely gets done because so many other job duties are on time constraints or help patrons immediately instead of in the long run. Show volunteers how to scan the shelves to make sure all of the fiction is arranged alphabetically by author's last name, then first name, then title. They will be able to catch any errors in shelving and align the books to look appealing as they do so. This task might involve more training in the nonfiction sections, but some volunteers might already understand the Dewey Decimal System and be willing to take on the challenge. If the library has any materials shelved on spinning racks, shelf reading is a huge help because they are only loosely alphabetized and can often get put back on the wrong rack, making them nearly impossible for patrons to find. In the case of group volunteers, several could tackle each fiction section (children, teen, adult), and a couple could help with the spinning racks.

Special projects can also be events the library holds or sponsors. If there is always a summer learning kickoff party at the beginning of June, make sure volunteers, service groups, and potential volunteers know the date and have an idea of some of the help that is needed. People who cannot or do not want to commit to a regular volunteer schedule might be more than willing to help out for one day or for one specific event. Some workplaces might even like to "adopt" a specific event the library puts on and help with it every time the event is held. Knowing that volunteers might like to be one-off helpers, library employees might feel more comfortable suggesting and planning special events. Instead of feeling like staff has to juggle all of the event job duties on top of their full-time jobs, they will have a pool of special event volunteers to mine for help and input. If the library wants to launch a new event, it might even be fun to get volunteers involved in the planning process. Since they will be helping the day of the event, they might like to have input as to how the event is set up. This means special groups can get more service hours, but if they are not able to meet in person, group emails or even a listserv can be set up so everyone's voice can be heard regardless of if they come to a meeting or not.

As library needs are assessed, keep big picture projects in mind because they can be assigned to groups and accomplished fairly quickly. After spreading the word about group service opportunities, the library might find that bigger projects initially just dreamed about can finally be made a reality due to the dedication of volunteers.

◎ Key Points

- Make a list of goals the library would achieve if there were no restrictions; volunteers will bring skills, dedication, and enthusiasm that can help these goals be met.
- How many volunteers will be able to work in the library? Consider its size and how many employees will also be working while volunteers are on duty.
- Write detailed job descriptions that will give volunteers an idea of what a task is before they take it on.

- Include the steps volunteers will do to finish the task, so they will be able to learn and complete work on their own.
- Make sure jobs are broken down into manageable tasks that can be easily completed during a volunteer shift.
- Have a list of special projects on the back burner so one-time volunteers or service groups can come to the library and complete tasks.
- Start small! Hire a few volunteers to kick off the volunteer program so they can be evaluated, tasks can be adapted, and volunteers can give quality feedback to help the program grow.

Launching the Volunteer Program

Applications

HAVING APPLICATIONS FOR VOLUNTEER POSITIONS helps the library learn about potential volunteers and keeping this information on file will help the program expand and change as new volunteers come in and new positions are created according to skills and interests. A simple application is best, with room for the applicant to fill in background and personal information. It is also a good idea to ask their availability up front, to see how they might fit in with the library's hours and with other volunteers. Asking about their interests and skills will help them get placed in the perfect position that will not only benefit the library, but also help the volunteer grow. If the library will always have a few volunteer jobs available, it is a good idea to list this on the application. Volunteers who mark that they would like to shelve books or prep for programs could be hired to come in regardless of their schedule availability, if this is something the library always needs help with.

An example application is given at the end of the book and can be adapted to include things certain organizations may ask of their volunteers on the front end. The volunteer application can be as long or as short as needed for individual organizations, but it is best to not overwhelm potential volunteers. Some might be applying to learn more about the library or the opportunity, which can more easily be done in an interview setting. A long, detailed application can turn away potential volunteers; it could be viewed as weeding out those who are not dedicated, but the application process should be the easiest part of bringing in volunteers. Looking over even simple applications will automatically weed out people who would not be a good fit for the library, and interviews can weed out even more. It is better to start with a large pool of applicants who have filled out a simple application because these applications will be quicker to scan. Create the application with this in mind: the volunteer coordinator will be looking over many applications, very quickly, and there should be certain answers that will flag a potential volunteer as a good fit or as an automatic no.

The application can be a single sheet of paper, or a piece of paper front and back. It can also be uploaded to the library's website as a printable PDF for patrons to access on their own or from library computers. Another option is to input the volunteer application information into a free survey tool, like SurveyMonkey.com or Google Forms (https://docs.google.com/forms/u/0/). People can apply from home, work, school, or inside the library without having to worry about printing the form and keeping up with it until they can return it to the library. The online applications can be sent directly to the volunteer coordinator's email address to be reviewed.

Hiring a lot of volunteers to jumpstart the program will be tempting, but it is better to thoroughly vet volunteers and kick off the program with fewer, high quality volunteers. It might be important to look at the times volunteers are available: would it be best for volunteers to work in the library during quiet weekday mornings, or is more help needed on weekend afternoons? If starting the program during the school year, is it more important for the library to give priority to students who need service hours? If so, send blank applications to high school guidance counselors and librarians and flag the completed applications when they come back. If shelving help is very needed, look for applications that mark that job as an interest, or look for people who have work experience in offices or list organizational skills.

Interviews

After the volunteer coordinator looks over applications, it is time to call people in for interviews. Some organizations skip this process, and instead just take on all volunteers who apply. For some organizations and some projects, this is an acceptable way to bring in volunteers. For example, if the library is having a Summer Learning Kick-Off and needs people to man crafts tables, just getting bodies to the library might be enough help. For ongoing volunteering, though, and to establish a strong volunteer program, it is important to interview volunteer candidates. The organization needs to treat volunteers seriously, just as incoming staff are treated. Showing volunteers that they are valued from the beginning will ensure they take their volunteer commitment seriously.

Some people applying for volunteer positions might already be active patrons of the library and might know the staff and their way around the library. But not everyone wanting to volunteer is familiar with the library and the employees, so it is a good idea to bring everyone in for an interview, even if they are a regular whom the staff loves. It is important to start every volunteer off on the same foot, so everyone has the same base knowledge about the library and the staff. This begins by having everyone apply with a paper or online application and having everyone come in for an initial interview.

Meeting potential volunteers face to face is important. In-person meetings can show a lot about a person, so it will give the volunteer coordinator an idea of how well the applicant might fit in with the library. The volunteer coordinator can see how comfortable the applicant seems inside the library, how confident they are at asking questions, and learn more about what the potential volunteer wrote on the application.

Keep in mind, when potentially hiring teen volunteers, that they might have not experienced an interview before. This does not mean that teens who do not return voicemails from the library need to be pursued, but the interviewer should be flexible with this process regarding teens. Whether an interview goes well or not, it can be a learning experience for the teen. Share with them what they did right, what can be improved, and give suggestions on how they can improve these behaviors. This includes having a professional outgoing message on said voicemail box! Give them tips on handshakes, greetings, answering interview questions thoughtfully, and more. If teens know they will get something out of the library's volunteer application process, word will get out and more teens will apply for this opportunity.

Create a list of questions to use when interviewing potential volunteers. This should be largely based on the job positions that are available for volunteers. If the application asked for information about scheduling availability and interest in certain positions, it can be a good jumping-off point for the interview. Having set interview questions for basic applicants does not mean that formula needs to be followed for every potential volunteer. It is best to tailor interview questions to the person's interest; in other words, do not ask if they can work mornings if they already marked that they can only volunteer on weekends. Do not ask if they would like to help with children's programs when they already wrote that they would prefer to shelve or work behind the scenes. Go into the interview with a knowledge about the person's background, availability, and interests from the application.

Stephen Ashley is a librarian living in North Carolina. He has worked with all ages in school, public, and special libraries, often serving as a volunteer coordinator in those libraries. Regarding potential volunteers, he has advice on what to look for.

There are a few qualities that are almost universally applicable. I would say the most important ones are flexibility, dedication, and independence.

Flexibility: Volunteers who can be flexible about the tasks they do, when they volunteer, and who they work with are ideal. Because tasks and priorities are constantly shifting, having volunteers who are willing to try out different things is a huge asset.

Dedication: Volunteers frequently perform tasks that are repetitive and generally less than glamorous. When volunteers still consistently put forth their best work, it is much appreciated. I find volunteers who have their own goals for their volunteer experience (i.e., wanting to learn more about the general functioning of a library or wanting to build their resume) are frequently more dedicated to their work.

Independence: Library staff can and should provide directions and guidelines to their volunteers, but sometimes staff get busy and volunteers need to complete tasks on their own. Volunteers who are able to solve problems and think logically about what they're doing (but also know when to ask questions) are great to have.[1]

This will help the volunteer coordinator cut to the chase and really find out if the volunteer will be a good worker for the library; likewise, the volunteer will learn if they will be a good fit for the library's needs.

Interviews can be formal or informal, depending on the library, the volunteer coordinator, and the overall attitude of the volunteer program. While it is important to strive for professionalism, volunteers are donating their time freely, so the guidelines do not need to be as strict for them as they are for employees. It is possible to seem conversational and personable with potential volunteers while still showing them that they are entering a professional organization and will be expected to give a commitment and work hard when they are on the clock.

Getting to know potential applicants during the interview process can also help the volunteer coordinator learn about what the library could offer, in terms of volunteer opportunities and library services and programming. Information like this can be learned from a few simple questions about what applicants have previously used the library for or what they are hoping to get out of their volunteer experience.

Volunteer Handbook

Creating a volunteer handbook is an involved task. It will take multiple drafts, countless revisions, and feedback from everyone associated with the program and the larger governing bodies outside of the library. It will be the most important piece of the volunteer program's foundation. It will have all the information volunteers need to get involved with the organization. It will have background information about the library and library system, details about how to apply and what qualifications are needed, job descriptions, and basically be a written support system for volunteers.

Keep in mind that this manual can be revised. After the program runs for a year, the handbook might be filled with notes that need to be implemented for the next phase. Summer might especially throw the program off base, so think about when to launch the program, and aim to start it during fall or spring, if possible.

The volunteer handbook will differ greatly if it is made for an entire library system as opposed to just one branch. There are ways to make it more personalized for each branch because staff knows their patrons, what information they would need to volunteer, and in what format they would like to read that information. Creating a program for the entire organization means things will be a bit more generalized. If this program is to be implemented across multiple branches, one broad handbook will give each branch a jumping off point and they can customize it for their population. Or, if they are too short staffed, they can use the program as it is and not need to do any work on their own turf. The handbook is the foundation of the volunteer program and will make it ready to implement in individual branches or over the library system as a whole.

Start the first draft of the volunteer handbook with an outline. Beginning with a broad outline gives room for things to be added as they come up or as employees think of them. Consider the basics that need to be covered, like dress code, professionalism, background checks, commitment, scheduling, and behaviors on the job. Job descriptions will be extremely detailed in the handbook and can include necessary forms, so the volunteers will have all the information together.

While it is a good idea to have separate copies of the volunteer applications to hand out to interested patrons to gauge interest before bestowing them with a hefty handbook, including such forms in the handbook ensure that potential volunteers have all the information in one place. They will be able to return forms after they have read all the job will entail and can commit to a task or schedule. This will not guarantee a commitment from a volunteer any more than a single piece of paper application, but it is worth including in the handbook to have everything volunteer-related in one place.

The rough outline will serve as a working table of contents for the handbook, which is a practical idea to feature at the beginning of the handbook. This gives volunteers and employees quick access to whatever information they might need. It also allows volunteers to read or reread sections they are interested in. If the handbook is posted online, the items in the table of contents can be linked to each section for immediate access.

Flesh out the beginning of the handbook with information about the library system, and the specific branch that the manual is for, if applicable. Have a short section about all the different libraries in the system so volunteers can become familiar with each, learn about new branches and neighborhoods, and possibly volunteer at various locations.

Include an encouraging note from the library's executive director or manager. Again, for specific branches it might be nice to have a more personal touch from the manager, but it is not necessary if it is not time- or cost-effective for the whole system.

Including a section about the rights and responsibilities of volunteers will help set the tone for the handbook and what is expected from the volunteers themselves. Think of what the library will offer volunteers: a preliminary interview, appropriate training, a safe environment to work, oversight from a helpful employee, a letter of recommendation, service hours for school or a project, personal fulfillment. Also mention what the library expects in return from their volunteer responsibilities: a certain commitment that can be discussed with the coordinator, participation in training, respect for staff and patrons, willingness to follow library guidelines, notice if they cannot make their shift or need to quit. These lists will be something volunteers can refer to as they read the further instructions in the handbook.

Also include the general guidelines expected of employees who work at the library. The dress code might not need to be enforced as much with volunteers as with paid employees, but overall the same basic things should be expected from someone who is giving their time compared to someone who is paid. Volunteers will rise to these expectations and take their roles more seriously, so it is important to have it all spelled out for them.

If volunteers should dress like employees, put that in the handbook. No short-shorts, no shirts with words on them, no ripped jeans—whatever the rules are, spell it out to make them clear. The dress code will segue nicely into behavior guidelines. Volunteers should act just as professional as staff, so that is easy to explain based on employee guidelines. How should volunteers interact with patrons, if at all? Should they help a patron find a book if they are shelvers who know the section they are in? Would it be better to empower volunteers to do this, or should the volunteer come to an employee, or simply direct the patron to the information desk? If volunteers can help patrons, should they be asked to limit conversations to library information only? It is important to not be too restrictive, but volunteers are there to work, so they do not need to give time to patrons who could be better helped by library employees.

Explaining how volunteers should interact with patrons is an important thing to bring up with employees. Would they rather let volunteers help patrons with minor questions and direct them to the information desk or circulation desk for other queries? Should all questions be directed to staff? Volunteers should not be giving incorrect information to patrons, so it is important to have the baseline of knowing when to answer a question and when to admit they are not sure of the answer and sending a patron to an employee.

If there are any guidelines about preferred language in your employee handbook, it is best to include it in the volunteer handbook too. Preferred language can include how to use person-first language when it comes to people with disabilities, like saying a woman has Down syndrome instead of saying "the Down syndrome woman" or other insensitive phrases. It is good to encourage volunteers to be welcoming and open to everyone, since they will encounter patrons as they perform their duties, and they will be spreading the word about the library and its volunteer program.

Are volunteers required to commit to the library? A year? Six months? A semester? The summer? It is important to outline this concept, so volunteers know what they are getting into. It is too much work to recruit, hire, and train volunteers just to have them quit after a week or two; that can be a huge drain on time and resources. It is also unfair to demand a commitment that volunteers will not be able to adhere to. Think about the potential volunteer population and what they might be able to do. Ask employees what they think a logical commitment would be. Ask patrons what they would be willing to commit to if they are interested in volunteering. It is important to always get feedback from the community. Mentioning commitment in the volunteer handbook will set the tone for the volunteers that apply to the library. They will understand that they are accepting a responsibility beyond just giving away a few hours of time here and there.

The discussion of commitment naturally leads to scheduling. With job descriptions figured out within the library or library system, it is easy to estimate how long each task should take. Shelving can be scheduled as two-hour blocks every weekday, or staggered shelving shifts on weekends. Prepping crafts for Saturday storytimes can be one two-hour shift after school. Cleaning picture books can be a four-hour session on Saturday afternoon, with plenty of breaks for volunteers to get a breath of fresh air.

Getting the schedule blocked off on the library's end will be the easiest part of scheduling. Filling the schedule with volunteers may take some time—and that is not just considering the application and hiring process. Finding committed volunteers who will stick to a schedule might be difficult. It is important to not get discouraged—as with most library work, it is important to be able to roll with the punches. If a volunteer does not show up for a shift, it should not be the end of the world, but it should be noted on the volunteer's evaluation sheet. Even if they called in ahead of time, keep a record of when they show up, when they call out, and when they pull a no-show.

Having a schedule for volunteers holds them accountable, plus they are more likely to show up when they know they have a day, a time, and a task to complete. Just dropping in when they have free time is nice—as bonus volunteer time, not as a way to always handle their volunteer hours. If volunteers call out for their shift but can reschedule before their next shift, always try to work with them if it does not place too much stress on the library. Being flexible is a major part of being able to retain volunteers. Ruling with an iron fist might mean volunteers quit before they get started. Do not be a pushover when it comes to scheduling and missing shifts but give volunteers a little more leeway than employees might get, since volunteers are donating their time.

Job descriptions will have their own large section. Each job should have a clear heading and detailed description. Jobs can be broken down further into the step-by-step training the employees have already developed.

Include information about liability and background checks in the handbook. Background checks may not be necessary for every volunteer, depending on their job duties, but it is a good idea to have all the information in the handbook so volunteers know what might be asked of them.

Liability will also vary, depending on the volunteers' tasks and the library or city's legal department. Make note of tasks that are risky—like shelving books in a crowded area, working with paper cutters, breathing in dust or cleaning chemicals—just so those working for the library's liability department know what they are dealing with and what the waivers need to cover.

Information about discipline and termination policies should be included in the handbook so volunteers will not feel targeted if they get scolded or fired. This is a great time to sit down with employees and get their feedback on this issue. Employees who have been resistant to the volunteer program in general will especially appreciate having their voices heard in this regard. They will have good ideas on how to effectively manage volunteers and behaviors. If certain employees seem totally resistant to volunteers, balance their feedback with that from other employees and find the middle ground of discipline.

What behaviors would cause a volunteer to be disciplined? Calling out repeatedly, showing up late, canceling shifts? What about how they interact with patrons? Would a patron complaint immediately be cause for dismissal, or would the volunteer be moved to a section that does not involve the public? Certainly, a volunteer found drinking alcohol or doing drugs would be terminated or engaging in inappropriate behavior by library standards. All of these policies should be fleshed out before you start the program, and if they are listed in the handbook, volunteers will not be surprised by any disciplinary actions that might come throughout their volunteer commitment.

Are the discipline standards the same for adult volunteers as they are for teen volunteers? In general, adult volunteers will act differently than teens. They are volunteering for different reasons—because they love the library, because they want to fill their time, because they volunteer with their friends. Teens usually volunteer for service hours for school, or to look good on college applications. Having different disciplinary actions for teens is not a bad idea, as long as everything is clearly spelled out in the handbook so there will be no disputes about preferential behaviors or the library being ageist.

Offer letters of recommendation for teen volunteers. This will ensure they take their volunteer duties seriously. It is often hard for teens to get a decent first job if they do not have any experience. Volunteering for a summer or keeping weekly shifts during the school year are great ways for them to show how dedicated they can be to a responsibility. Highlight the letters of recommendation when promoting the volunteer program to teens, on high school visits, and talking to counselors and club leaders who might be interested in service hours. The letters could be a great perk to pull in teen volunteers.

Letters of recommendation can also be a perk for transitional volunteers—those who are between jobs or trying to find a new career. Make this possibility clear when interviewing volunteers; they might take their commitment more seriously if they know they are getting something tangible out of it.

Does the library employ a "three strikes, you're out" policy, or hand out pink slips? If a volunteer is repeatedly being disciplined, when will the library let them go? A volunteer who is acting out or not performing their job duties is a drain on the library. Rowdy or unprofessional volunteers will also make the library look bad, so that needs to be considered as well.

The handbook should be something volunteers can keep for their records, so it needs to be cost effective for the library. Do not create a 200-page document that needs to be perfect bound—no library can afford that, and no volunteer wants to read that. On the other hand, do not hand volunteers one sheet of paper and expect them to take the program seriously. It is important to find the balance of the perfect way to give volunteers the information they need and convey the seriousness of the program while making sure the handbooks are something your library can easily create and distribute.

If an online handbook seems like it would work better for the library's volunteer population, it could definitely be done. Give patrons a card with a link or QR code printed on it that will lead them to the handbook on the library's website. Link the handbook and volunteer application form on the website, feature it prominently, and promote it to in-person and online patrons.

◎ Training

Having the job duties written out thoroughly will help determine what training is required for each task. Employees wrote out these job descriptions, so they can also help figure out what training needs to be done. Make sure this idea is presented to employees in a meeting with a chance for them to speak their mind. They might prefer to train a volunteer to do their tasks directly, to make sure it will be done a certain way. Or they might prefer to be more hands-off, just writing up guidelines for the handbook and coordinator to access. Either way, make sure employees are encouraged to be active in this process. This is the foundation of the volunteer program, and it is important to make it as strong as possible. Even if employees want to be hands off when it comes to the volunteers themselves, they can help with this aspect of it and still feel like a major part of the team.

Stephen Ashley is a librarian in North Carolina who has worked as a volunteer coordinator with all ages in school, public, and special libraries. When it comes to training volunteers, he has some input:

> Volunteer coordination takes up a lot of time. Because volunteers work when they're able and don't spend the same amount of time working as staff, I spent a lot of time on scheduling and re-explaining tasks and procedures. It helps a lot when other library staff is willing to get to know volunteers and help them out, particularly if you have volunteers coming in after you've left for the day. It's also helpful when as much of your program is automated as possible (i.e., there's a specific procedure for signing up to volunteer, letting people know about scheduling issues, there's a place for people to re-read policies and procedures, etc.).[2]

Training can be written up in the volunteer handbook, but training sessions will need to be held for volunteers. Just as detailed job descriptions can tell volunteers what is expected of them, a detailed training section will tell them how to reach their, and the library's, goals. Written descriptions are no substitute for seeing how a job is done in the library. Think about how many volunteers will be in the library, and how often. Volunteer training sessions could either be held in orientation groups, or one on one as new volunteers start. Scheduling training depends on the volunteer coordinator's workload and what other activities will be going on at the library.

Some jobs might be able to be combined into the same training sessions; people assigned to shelving can come in at the same time for a brief orientation. For tasks like shelving, there are other ways to train and test volunteers. There are online videos about shelving in different departments, and online tests where volunteers can shelve a stack of virtual books. The library could even create its own orientation videos, either with the volunteer coordinator, or volunteers themselves!

Teen volunteers love working with photos and videos and might be willing to help create training videos as their volunteer hours. These are great ways volunteer opportunities can come up organically. If the library wants to feature custom volunteer orientation videos, reach out to local high schools. A video club might be willing to help, or a beta club whose members need service hours. Partnerships like this can be mutually beneficial—think outside the box!

LRNG is an organization that proposes using playlists for learning (https://www .lrng.org/playgroundcity/badge/playlist). Potential volunteers can watch videos relevant to library duties on a library computer before they start their first task. In this context, a playlist is like a list of information needed for a task, except in the form of videos for accessible learning. The tasks are more engaging and interactive, without a volunteer coordinator having to oversee every step of the learning process. Once a playlist is viewed and the tasks are completed, volunteers earn a badge, which could help keep track of volunteers in your library. Volunteers could "level up" as they view more playlists, become more familiar with the library, and put in active volunteer hours. These badges could help when it comes time to reward volunteers for their investment or help determine which volunteers are senior enough to train newcomers.

Playlists can be made for any task: shelving, prepping program supplies, cleaning books, and more. The library can make its own videos, or they can be found online. Simple videos with text instructions are fairly simple to create and can be more engaging than text on plain paper. Putting work into the front end of volunteer training might help volunteers see how invested the library is in the program and their skills, so it is worth taking a little extra time to get this done.[3]

If the library does not want to use LRNG playlists, think about the orientations. If time management is a concern with the library, then holding set orientation sessions might be best. Hold one for teens on the first Saturday of the month. Have adult volunteers come in on a Monday evening once a month. Think about what works best for the volunteers, and when the volunteer coordinator can spare some time. Think of what tasks can be shown together without confusing volunteers about their job duties. It does not hurt volunteers to know how other aspects of the library work, even if they will not be shelving. Go over the basics of shelving after conducting a tour of the library, and everyone can learn. Get volunteers started shelving and take the others on to their assigned jobs and specialized orientations.

Make sure volunteers know they can always ask questions. Volunteers shelving especially need to know this, because if a book is mis-shelved in the library, it is virtually lost. If they are not exactly sure where a book goes, they can ask and learn. Make sure training videos or playlists are always accessible; keep them bookmarked on a library computer volunteers can use. Keep the volunteer handbook in an accessible place next to the volunteer sign-in sheet so they can look back over training and see helpful hints written in the handbook.

Training is not just a one-time thing; it is not just a two-hour orientation. Training is ongoing, and it is important to check in with volunteers periodically, and possibly have them go over training tasks even if they have been completed previously. Consider how involved the volunteers need to be; they could be included in staff meetings that cover relevant topics. Planning to move the graphic novels from nonfiction to a separate section in front is a big task, and while library employees really need to make the decision, volunteers could chime in. They might be doing the bulk of the moving process, and they might have some input about how frequently they shelve those books, or how often they are asked for the genre's location while they are in the stacks.

Training includes volunteer evaluations; take what you see the volunteers doing and turn it into learning experiences, so they can grow their skills. Get their input on what they need to know more about, or what they think might improve the branch. Volunteers are a unique group: they are coming in as free help, but they are invested in the library because that is where they choose to give their time. Even if they were not previously patrons of the library, they care about the library as soon as they start volunteering, because things that affect the library will affect their duties and workload.

⊚ Key Points

- Job duties should be spelled out clearly, so volunteers know what is expected of them and have steps to show them how they can perform the job.
- In addition to the steps written in the job duties, volunteer training should include in-person orientations and shadowing sessions.
- Consider recording videos of training sessions so volunteers can watch them on demand. Teen volunteers or audio-visual clubs might be a good resource when it comes to creating custom videos.
- The volunteer handbook is an important document for the library and volunteers. Make sure it has all the information volunteers need to have on the front end and let them keep a copy so they can reference them as needed.
- Put the volunteer handbook online if possible, so volunteers can easily access it at no cost to the library.
- Remember that training is not a one-time orientation. It will take time and practice for volunteers to learn their new jobs. Be available for comments and questions and consider ways to help volunteers feel more comfortable doing their tasks.

⊚ Notes

1. "Interview with Stephen Ashley." Email interview by author. July 16, 2018.
2. "Interview with Stephen Ashley." Email interview by author. July 16, 2018.
3. "LRNG | About." LRNG. Accessed May 24, 2018. https://www.lrng.org/about.

⊚ References

"Interview with Stephen Ashley." Email interview by author. July 16, 2018.
"LRNG | About." LRNG. Accessed May 24, 2018. https://www.lrng.org/about.

Volunteer Program Foundations

ⓖ Adult Volunteers

ADULT VOLUNTEERS TYPICALLY FORM the bulk of a volunteer program. They are adults who are invested in the library and the community, seniors who have time to give to organizations they care about, and college students who need service hours for scholarships or class credit. Adult volunteers usually have more flexibility with their schedule and can help at times when teen or children volunteers are unavailable due to school and other commitments. Adult volunteers can also help with the biggest variety of tasks.

Job Duties

Adults can help with more around the library because they usually have more flexible schedules, knowledge, and strength than younger volunteers. This gives them a wider variety of job duties to choose from. Adult volunteers can do a lot of tasks that library staff do, freeing up library staff to help more with customers or get ahead with programming plans and other work.

Many library duties take place behind the scenes to help the library run smoothly. Books need to be shelved, lost books need to be searched for, older books need to be cleaned and repaired, and more. With library staff helping patrons, these tasks often fall to the wayside, and as a result, the library does not look as polished as it could. When volunteers complete some of the behind the scenes tasks, they take ownership in the library and feel pride in the building and their community. Feeling productive and a part of something larger than them also gives volunteers a positive view of the library. They will share their experience with others via word of mouth, which is a great way to get free publicity for the library—and possibly recruit more volunteers.

Adults have different backgrounds and experiences that will enable them to help the library in countless ways. After interviewing and hiring adult volunteers, get input on what job duties they think they would enjoy and could complete well, but also ask what job duties they were envisioning when they decided to volunteer at the library. Some volunteers might just want to shelve books, so they can see the titles available or feel like part of something bigger. Other volunteers might have big ideas of what they could accomplish with the library, so it is important to listen to their input and see what volunteer jobs could be created. If nothing else, volunteers will have a fresh viewpoint and an outsider's perspective of the library and what it could be. These volunteers are stakeholders in the library, members of the community, and it is important to value their input, even if it is just putting ideas away for later use.

Job duties for adult volunteers will be written out in the volunteer handbook, so they will always have an opportunity to read over the steps to refresh their memories, and they will always know what is expected of them. If volunteers are assigned certain duties, reading other job descriptions may inspire them to help in other areas or mix up their volunteer shifts slightly. Try to be flexible enough to allow volunteers to try different things. It will help everyone involved to have volunteers learning how to accomplish every available task; they can fill in for missing volunteers, pick up extra shifts in other areas, or just feel more like part of the team. Learning how other volunteer jobs are done might help volunteers do their own work more efficiently or might inspire them to propose other job duties to the volunteer coordinator.

Orientation

When interviewing potential volunteers, a library tour is advised. However, it is a good idea to tour the library again at a volunteer orientation. Depending on the volunteer coordinator's schedule and the volunteers' schedules, it might work to have a group orientation one evening after office hours, or on a weekend afternoon. For group orientations, tour all of the volunteers around the library. Identify each section of the library and explain what jobs will be done there. For example, "This is the Children's section. Fiction chapter books are here, and picture books are here; both are shelved in alphabetical order by author's last name. Children's nonfiction books are here, arranged by Dewey Decimal classification number. Volunteer shelvers work in this section, and children's programs are also held here on Saturday mornings. Volunteers can help prepare for programs, assist with crafts after storytime, and help clean up when the program is over." Giving volunteers a lot of information as they tour will help them see the scope of the library and realize how each section fits into the larger picture, as well as get an idea of the jobs they can volunteer to do. This will also allow them to ask questions; even if the answers are in the handbook or will come later on the tour, it's good to address questions as they arise. "How does the Dewey Decimal System work?" a volunteer may ask, and the volunteer coordinator can answer along the lines of, "Nonfiction books are grouped by subject and assigned a number; we will go over it in detail later in orientation or when shelvers start their training."

Details given during the tour will vary according to the library's setup, the scope of the volunteer program, and how many volunteers are on each tour. On smaller orientation tours, the volunteer coordinator might prefer to be more specific with information that relates to the volunteers listening, and it might be easier to address questions as they come up. Larger orientation tours are also fine; it might work better to tour more volunteers around the library at once, get them started with brief trainings on sample tasks, and check in to see how they are doing. Any further training can be given one-on-one or in pairs for volunteers completing the same jobs.

If the volunteer coordinator's schedule allows, having individual orientations on each volunteer's first day could be an effective way of onboarding. The volunteer coordinator could show the volunteer around the library, briefly introduce the various job duties, and have the volunteer shadow a staff member who is currently doing that task. This way, volunteers will meet a library employee, see how they do their job as a professional, and try their hand at the task with a skilled worker watching. This will help the volunteer get immediate feedback on their work while letting them see how the task fits into the bigger picture of the library's workings.

Volunteer orientations can be led in a variety of ways, and there is not really a wrong way to do it as long as volunteers are becoming familiar with the library, are seeing how various jobs are done, and have a chance to ask questions. Since the orientation is just the first day, or even held before the volunteer's initial work shift, there will be plenty of time for the volunteer to learn and ask more questions, give feedback to the library and the volunteer coordinator, and expand their volunteer position.

Scheduling

Scheduling adult volunteers is usually straightforward and can be the easiest part of the volunteer coordinator's job. Adult volunteers typically have more set schedules than teens or college students, so they can commit to a certain schedule each month. Instances may come up where adult volunteers have to call out of their shifts, but overall they are reliable volunteers and should be asked to keep a regular commitment.

Specific scheduling can be done by the volunteer coordinator, depending on the individual volunteers. If a volunteer can work every Monday morning, they can be scheduled for that shift regardless of what work is available. When the volunteer arrives on Monday morning, they can shelve books that were returned over the weekend, or help check in the bookdrop, or help set up the meeting rooms for that day's events. On the other hand, if a volunteer only wants to shelve books, their prime shifts might be evenings after the bookdrop has been brought in and library workers are busy with closing duties. If the shelving volunteer is coming in on Monday evening, it is better to have the Monday morning volunteer not shelving, to ensure the regular volunteer will have their task.

Details like this might take a little juggling, but it is manageable. Keeping one major calendar—a paper desk calendar or an accessible and editable online calendar—for adult volunteers can help keep everyone on the same page. Input volunteer names for the shift times they prefer, then make notes about what they will be doing. The Monday evening 4:00pm–7:00pm shift, for example, can be marked with the volunteer's name and "Shelving." That way, the Monday morning shift can either be assigned another duty on the calendar so the volunteer knows what to do without needing in-person guidance, or they can look to see that a shelver is coming in later, so they will not need to do that task. Similarly, a checklist for each day or week can be kept next to the volunteer sign-in desk.

The list can have all of the available volunteer duties, and volunteers can initial next to the task they will be doing during their shift. If a shelving volunteer is coming in on certain days, put their initials next to that task before the sheet is put out, so other volunteers will know that job is accounted for. Empowering volunteers to structure their own work shifts will help make them independent workers who feel like an important part of the library team. Instead of standing around waiting for someone to show them what needs to be done, they will be able to sign in for their shift, look over the available tasks, pick one to complete, and get to work.

Once the volunteers have been coming in for a few weeks, they will be able to manage their own schedules easily and will likely only contact the volunteer coordinator if they have to miss a shift, or if they need to drastically change their work days. This means that a bit of effort on the front end, setting up the calendar schedule and creating a task list template, will free up the volunteer coordinator to work on the program in other ways, such as making sure volunteers are successful at their jobs, and brainstorming how to grow the program.

Checking In

The volunteer coordinator should regularly check in with volunteers to see how they are enjoying their tasks, if they feel they can complete them adequately with the time and resources given. After a few shifts, volunteers might realize that they are not able to shelve all of the adult fiction books in two hours. The volunteer might feel like they have let the library down by not finishing their task or might rush and make mistakes to finish the task in the allotted time. Checking in with volunteers and hearing this type of feedback will help the volunteer coordinator see that two volunteers need to work the shelving shift, or that the job of shelving adult fiction books should be split into two separate tasks of shelving A–M books, and shelving N–Z books. The volunteer might also have good ideas about how the task can be adapted to be completed easily.

Checking in will also give volunteers a chance to ask questions. They might have misunderstood the job duty during orientation or learned a wrong step during training. It is not vital to check in during every volunteer shift, but it is not a bad idea to be available to volunteers that frequently. Check ins should definitely happen after the first shift, and one soon after, just to make sure the volunteer is doing the task correctly and feels comfortable doing it. Checking in several times at the beginning of their commitment will also make the volunteer realize that the library wants them to succeed and is available to help them. This will empower the volunteers to come to the coordinator with questions and suggestions.

Checking in also includes asking the volunteer if they enjoy their job duties. A shelver might have wanted to shelve books to see what the library has to offer and keeps checking out several books at the end of their shifts. They might get tired of this task or feel overwhelmed with how they cannot resist checking out more books and want to try something else. The good thing is, they do not have to worry about spending their paycheck at the library! They are volunteering for free, but are able to check out for free, so it is a win-win situation. Regardless, they might want to try helping with programming instead, just to mix up their shifts. If the coordinator does not check in, this volunteer might start feeling burned out about their volunteer experience and quit altogether, not knowing that switching positions is an option.

Keeping tabs on volunteers by checking in regularly will also help the coordinator evaluate the volunteers. Brief notes can be made for the volunteer's file after each check in, dated, so the volunteer coordinator can remember how to best help that volunteer the next time they come. For example, after speaking with the shelver who wants to change positions, the volunteer coordinator can make a brief note of this. When reviewing the volunteer's file before the next shift, the coordinator will remember to train the volunteer on the new position and get them started with it. Similarly, these check ins and job changes might affect the volunteer's schedule, so the coordinator will need these notes to ensure that the volunteer is coming in during a time when program help is needed, instead of still coming in at a time for shelving when no program is scheduled.

Expanding the Job

The process of checking in with volunteers will also help the volunteer coordinator expand the volunteer program. Though the library and the volunteer coordinator created the volunteer program, it is the volunteers themselves who will help sustain it, while pushing to expand.

Volunteers who help with program prep see what goes into planning and setting up a library program. They often stay at the program to be an extra set of hands and help take it down when it is over. They also do not usually have a library background, so they are coming at library programs with an outsider's point of view. This means they might start to get ideas for good programs the library could offer. They might also hear what patrons are saying as they leave a program, meaning they are hearing feedback the library could use to change up their programming. In fact, having volunteers who help with programming ask attendees for feedback would be a great way to use their time. Patrons might feel more comfortable being honest with a volunteer, whom they might view as an equal, as opposed to feeling like they need to only give positive feedback to library employees.

Adult volunteers have various backgrounds and experiences to pull from when they come to volunteer. Someone might be a retired accountant who would love to lead a tax help program. Someone might be an artist who wants to lead a painting class. Writers might volunteer to have writing workshops. Letting volunteers suggest program topics, and even lead the programs themselves, will empower them and encourage them to get more involved in the library. If the program idea seems like a good fit for the library, and an employee can help with the program, it is worth giving it a try. The library might be surprised at the different people or number of people who come through the doors for something new.

The bottom line of the volunteer program is that it will be sustainable as long as the volunteer coordinator is checking in with volunteers and keeping them active. When volunteers feel supported, they will continue to donate their time to an organization. The extra step of giving volunteers freedom in their job positions and being flexible with what they want to do is what will allow the volunteer program to grow and expand. The volunteers do not need to have total control over the program, but if they feel empowered to take responsibility, then they will be able to maintain the program with little oversight from the coordinator, freeing the coordinator to develop the program from other angles.

◎ Teen Volunteers

Teen volunteers are typically middle school students and high school students, ranging in age from twelve to eighteen. Younger volunteers will be classified as children, and older will be classified as adult, even if they are teenaged college students.

Teenagers might only volunteer because they need service hours for school, or because their parents are making them get out of the house. Regardless of the reason behind their volunteering, they are still valuable volunteers. They might have innovative ideas about how the library can stay relevant in the community and with their peers. They may also have different ideas about programming, promotion, and even interacting with patrons inside the library. Teen volunteers might help with the library's social media outlets, doing an Instagram volunteer takeover for a day, or help patrons with tech questions so the reference librarians are freed up to help with other queries.

Teen volunteers, regardless of their reason for volunteering, can all gain work experience from a volunteer position. Make this clear to volunteers before they start; if they know the library sees this as a serious position, they will be more likely to take it seriously. Treat them like mature employees but keep in mind they are teenagers and might have more issues interfering with volunteering. It might be harder for them to get to and from the library for shifts; school activities or other events might crop up on short notice, forcing a teen volunteer to call out of a shift. Since it's a volunteer position and a learning experience, it is best to have a little leeway with teens in certain areas, but to keep the overall level of the program professional. Each individual library will have to think about what they value in the program and about teens, what the library wants to get from teen volunteers, and what the library wants teen volunteers to get from the library experience.

Summer Volunteers

Working with teen volunteers during the summer is usually easier than working with school year volunteers, just because there is more leeway for scheduling volunteer shifts, and often more jobs to be done around the library. If it is possible for the library to pick when to launch the volunteer program, or at least the teen volunteer program, summer is a great time to get it started. More time for volunteers and more jobs for them to do means the volunteers will feel more valued and have a great experience at the library. They will be more likely to want to volunteer again next summer, or even keep volunteering with reduced hours during the school year. They will spread the word about the library's positive volunteer experience to their friends and classmates, which will help the teen volunteer program grow. Parents will be pleased that their teens had a great summer earning quality work experience at a community organization and will also spread the word and perhaps even want to volunteer themselves.

Keep all of this in mind when developing the teen volunteer program but remember that not too many teen volunteers need to be hired to start the program. Having too many teens might make it difficult to juggle schedules, find jobs, and keep everyone busy all summer. Think of the library's needs and decide how many teens will be able to help with what duties and hire volunteers accordingly. Keep in mind the coverage needed throughout the day, and make sure teen volunteers are equally available in the mornings, afternoons, and evenings. Families might also take vacations during the summer, and teens will have to take time off accordingly. A different application for teen summer volunteers might make the hiring process easier; have an expanded section for scheduling availability so teens feel comfortable selecting the times they can work. Ask them to list any prior commitments, like classes, other volunteer work or paying jobs, family obligations, and more. This will help the volunteer coordinator hire teens who can be reliable throughout the summer months.

The library can decide if it is necessary for summer teen volunteers to have a handbook; it might not be necessary for such a short commitment. Summer volunteer positions are usually more about jumping in and helping out as opposed to a volunteer being onboarded and learning their position to grow over time. Instead of a handbook, a single page or a page front and back of detailed job descriptions might be enough. Hand this list out at the orientations and keep a few copies at the volunteer sign-in station so it will always be accessible for reference. Including a list of bullet points about how teen volunteers are to dress and behave could also substitute for a volunteer handbook during the summer months.

Job Duties

Teens are capable of helping in the library in many different ways, but for summer volunteers it is best to pick a few jobs and have teens sign up for shifts. Typically, a lot of teens will need a lot of hours in the summer, either to keep busy, get work experience, or fulfill service hours for school or the community. Instead of having too many teens doing too many jobs in the library each day, pick how many jobs will need to be done each day and how many teens are needed to complete those tasks.

For example, a mid-sized library branch might need a teen to help with a Summer Learning table and two teens to shelve children's and young adult books every weekday. These jobs are also available on Saturdays, with an additional teen helping at the Summer Learning table, and two teens to help with program prep and clean up. From here, break the day down into shifts. How long is the library open? Does the day break down evenly into three three-hour shifts? How long can teens work before they need a break? Would it work best for the library to have shifts of different teens coming in thrice a day, or would it be more efficient to have two shifts of teens, but include a short lunch or snack break? This depends on the library's size, hours, and number of teens needing hours, but an effective program can be created regardless of how teens' summer shifts are structured.

Once the hours are decided, calculate how many shifts teens can sign up for each week. Depending on how many teen volunteers are hired, it might only be fair to allow them to sign up for two shifts a week. In an ideal library, it would be great if teens could sign up for one shift of each task every week—referring back to the previous example, that would be one shelving shift, one Summer Learning table shift, and one program help shift. Letting teens take on different job duties will turn them into more well-rounded volunteers for the library, make them feel more involved with the library overall, and show them how much there is to do at the library, which will hopefully bring them back to volunteer next summer. As a bonus, trying out different jobs will help prepare them for future work experiences.

Job duties should be both written and verbally explained clearly, in terms the teens can understand, and demonstrated whenever possible. Depending on what the library decides about a summer volunteer handbook, job descriptions can be listed on a single sheet of paper for volunteers to take home or kept on hand at the sign-in desk. The bulk of job demonstration can be done during the orientation and will be addressed in that section.

Orientation

Schedule two or three orientation sessions at different times for summer volunteers. A weekday evening, a weekend morning, a weekend afternoon—whatever works for the teen population. Putting a few options on the application will give an idea of what will work with teens' schedules before anything is put on the calendar. Teens should sign up for the orientation they know they can attend, and this should be treated as vital to their volunteer commitment. Some teen volunteer programs make it a requirement that teens attend an orientation session before they can volunteer, which is not a bad idea to kick off the teen program on a serious note. Keep records for teen volunteers; a simple checklist of all that volunteers are required to turn in and attend will be enough. A list with room for checkmarks and notes about the application, interview, orientation, schedule set, missed shifts, job performance, and more will help the volunteer coordinator remember how each volunteer performed. Even brief notes will help at the end of summer when the coordinator is writing recommendation letters.

Teen volunteer orientations should be informative and to the point, with time for questions and scheduling at the end of the session. Teens can be gathered as a group to be given general information about volunteering, such as the importance of commitment, the dress code, the way to schedule shifts, how to call out, and anything else that will apply to everyone. Any printed information should be directly handed to each teen to ensure they get a copy, as opposed to passing a stack around the room. Have a table set up with handouts and a sign out sheet for teens to confirm they received copies of everything. Give them a few minutes to look over the printed materials and then ask for questions, because as the information sinks in, they might think of something to ask that will benefit the group.

If teen summer volunteers are able to sign up for all different tasks, then the orientation should devote time to job demonstrations. If teens need to pick one job to do all summer, make this clear before the jobs are demonstrated so they can pay attention and pick a task they will be able to stick with. Take teens on a tour of the library first, to give them an overview of how the library is arranged, where they will sign in and out for shifts, and where they can take breaks, if break time is included in their shifts. After exploring the whole library, go back to relevant areas to explain job duties. For example, in the young adult and children's sections, explain how books are shelved and how to keep shelves looking nice. From here, go to where the returned books needing to be shelved are kept. Depending on group size, each volunteer could even pick a book, take it back to the shelves, shelve it, and let the volunteer coordinator look it over to make sure it was correctly placed. If the groups are too large, keeping shelving tests and experience on the back burner until each volunteer's first shift is acceptable.

Once the tour is complete and the jobs have been demonstrated in the relevant areas, take teens back to the original orientation room. Briefly explain the available jobs once more so they will have each task fresh on their minds when it comes time to schedule shifts.

Scheduling

One of the most straightforward ways to schedule teen volunteers in the summer is to have a huge desk calendar for each month, for each job, such as: a June calendar for the Summer Learning Table, a June calendar for the Program Help, and a June calendar for Shelving. Make three calendars exactly like this for July. A little prep on the front end will make this an effective scheduling tool: black out days the library is closed and block off the shifts on each calendar, for example 10:00am–1:00pm, 1:00pm–4:00pm, 4:00pm–7:00pm. If two teens can work for certain shifts, put numbers one and two in the empty spaces so teens know two volunteers are needed.

June Teen Volunteers: Summer Learning Table

Sunday	Monday	Tuesday	Wednesday	Thursday	Friday	Saturday
					1	2
3	4 10a-1p 1p-4p 4p-7p	5 10a-1p 1p-4p 4p-7p	6 10a-1p 1p-4p 4p-7p	7 10a-1p 1p-4p 4p-7p	8 10a-1p 1. 2. 1p-4p 1. 2. 4p-7p 1. 2.	9 10a-1p 1. 2. 1p-4p 1. 2. 4p-7p 1. 2.
10	11 10a-1p 1p-4p 4p-7p	12 10a-1p 1p-4p 4p-7p	13 10a-1p 1p-4p 4p-7p	14 10a-1p 1p-4p 4p-7p	15 10a-1p 1. 2. 1p-4p 1. 2. 4p-7p 1. 2.	16 10a-1p 1. 2. 1p-4p 1. 2. 4p-7p 1. 2.
17	18 10a-1p 1p-4p 4p-7p	19 10a-1p 1p-4p 4p-7p	20 10a-1p 1p-4p 4p-7p	21 10a-1p 1p-4p 4p-7p	22 10a-1p 1. 2. 1p-4p 1. 2. 4p-7p 1. 2.	23 10a-1p 1. 2. 1p-4p 1. 2. 4p-7p 1. 2.
24	25 10a-1p 1p-4p 4p-7p	26 10a-1p 1p-4p 4p-7p	27 10a-1p 1p-4p 4p-7p	28 10a-1p 1p-4p 4p-7p	29 10a-1p 1. 2. 1p-4p 1. 2. 4p-7p 1. 2.	30 10a-1p 1. 2. 1p-4p 1. 2. 4p-7p 1. 2.

Figure 5.1. Monthly desk calendars for each volunteer job give teens an easy way to schedule summer volunteer shifts.

Volunteers will sign up in the empty blocks on different job calendars, so they will know what they are doing, when. They can write down their shifts before they leave orientation or snap a picture with their phones.

Before letting teens anywhere near the calendars, make sure the scheduling guidelines are clear. Can they sign up for two shifts a week? If so, do they need to do the same job both shifts, or can they try different positions? Is there a minimum time requirement for teens? Do they need to have at least one shift every week? Keep in mind teens may be going on vacations during the summer and might have to miss a week; more general requirements like ten shifts over the entire summer might be better than requesting them to work every week. Also consider how to juggle the shifts; teens love to sleep late when possible, and go out at night, so it might be difficult to fill the morning and evening time slots. It is not fair for a handful of teens to monopolize all of the afternoon shifts. On the other hand, some teens might have prior morning or evening commitments. These issues, along with any vacation time, can and should be discussed during the interview, if not addressed on the application itself.

Once teens have scheduled their summer shifts and written it down or taken photos for their own reference, have them check with the volunteer coordinator before leaving. The volunteer can give a brief rundown of their schedule and mention their first day of work so the volunteer coordinator has a general idea of who is doing what, as well as ensuring the volunteer understands their schedule and the commitment.

Accountability and Rewards

Starting with the application process, it should be clear that the library expects teens to be hard workers and act professionally. While they are not getting compensated financially for their time, teens will be earning service hours as well as letters of recommendation and references for other jobs and opportunities, and they should be aware of this ahead of time. The volunteer coordinator will be responsible for these recommendations and will have to be honest, so teens should know that while their strengths will be highlighted, it will be noted if they do things like dress unprofessionally or miss shifts without notice.

Having teens sign in and out for each shift is a must. They need to get used to being on time and being responsible for marking that time. If breaks are permitted, teens should sign in and out for breaks also. A teen forgetting to sign in should not mean that they do not get credit for their shift because they are learning about the work environment through this experience, but make sure a great importance is put on the act of signing in and out on time. Once the habit is instilled with the first few shifts, it will be mindless, and teens will do it without thinking.

Table 5.1. Teen volunteers need to learn to sign in and out every shift to get credit for their volunteer hours.

DATE	VOLUNTEER'S NAME	TIME IN	TIME OUT	TOTAL TIME WORKED

The volunteer coordinator should keep records for each volunteer regarding the shifts they work and how much they complete during their shift. Checking in with teen volunteers is much more important than with adult volunteers, mostly to let them know they are being held accountable. Showing up for a shift and hanging out in the library for two or three hours does not count as volunteering; doing the work is what counts as volunteering. There is no need to pressure teens to finish all of the library's tasks during their shift, but they do need to accomplish what is a reasonable amount of work for that time.

It is also important to keep records about teens calling out for their shifts. While calling out with advance notice is the responsible thing to do, it can be done too often, making the volunteer unreliable to the library. Calling out moments before the shift is to begin is even more unreliable, unless they are calling about being delayed due to car trouble, within reason.

Teens will be rewarded by earning service hours for their schools or community organizations, as well as having a work experience to reference on resumes and applications, accompanied by a letter of recommendation. These alone make participating in the volunteer program valuable to teens, but offering other incentives can be a good idea, depending on how the library feels about incentives overall. Some libraries have moved away from offering incentives for summer reading challenges with mixed results, so if the library does

Table 5.2.   Individual volunteer pages give volunteer coordinators a place to keep a running total of hours worked, as well as notes about the volunteer's performance, schedule, or any questions that arise.

VOLUNTEER'S NAME _____   **MONTH** _____

DATE	HOURS WORKED	NOTES

not offer reading incentives, it would be in keeping with the organization to not offer additional volunteer incentives. However, incentives do not always have to be prizes.

Teens who do not miss a shift and complete a reasonable amount of work during each shift should be empowered to take on leadership roles within the program. This might mean they are eligible to take on more shifts if they need more hours or want more experience. This might mean that they have first choice when it comes to school year volunteer shifts. This might mean that they get to take a break on the clock once a week. The rewards can be decided on by the volunteer coordinator and library staff, because the volunteers need to feel valued, but also their new roles and responsibilities need to benefit the library as a whole, not become another task for the coordinator to oversee.

School Year Volunteers

If the library starts the teen volunteer program during the summer, it is a good idea to ask the volunteers if they would like to continue during the school year. Depending on how many tasks are available during the school year (for example, the Summer Learning table jobs would not be available) and how long the library is open outside of school hours, the volunteer coordinator might only ask certain volunteers if they would like a school year position. This goes back to the reward system the library might want to employ.

If the teen volunteer program is starting during the school year, teen patrons can be asked in person if they would like to volunteer after school. Information about the program and applications can be given to counselors, librarians, and teachers at local high schools. These adults can vet the students before the applications even make it to the volunteer coordinator, which will save time by letting the library know that these potential volunteers are responsible and interested in juggling this position on top of their school commitments. These volunteers can then be offered jobs during the next summer volunteer session, so once the program gets started, it will be relatively easy to cycle volunteers around to make sure the library always has teen help.

Public Library

Teens volunteering at the public library during the school year will have a limited schedule, and job duties should not be too involved, in consideration of everything else on their plates. If possible, it is a good idea for the volunteer coordinator and library management to give school year volunteers a little more flexibility with their schedules. Student volunteers might have to call out on short notice if a major school project comes up. Some students might even be juggling a paying job on top of school and volunteering at the library to earn service hours. Keeping this in consideration, it might be best if teen volunteer duties during the school year are things that are not vital to the library or can be done by other volunteers if a stretch of time goes by with teen volunteers being unable to come in to work.

Job Duties

Students volunteering during the school year are limited in what they can do and when they are available, so it is best to maximize the time they can donate to the library. Having multiple volunteer stations set up helps teens know what they can do when. During the school year, it is ideal for library staff to pull all books teens can shelve and keep them in a central location, for example keeping all Young Adult books to be shelved on a cart right near the Young Adult section of the library. This empowers teens to sign in for their shift and go right to the section and get to work, instead of patrolling the library to see what needs to be done. Shelving is a job duty that can be done regardless of how much time teens can dedicate to the library. Even if they are coming in for thirty minutes while they wait to be picked up after school, they can sign in, shelve a few books, and earn some volunteer time.

One volunteer station that is always a hit is a card-making station. This can be set up at the back of the reference desk, at an empty table in the study section, at a counter in the employee workroom, or even on a portable cart volunteers can pull supplies from. Blank cards and paper can be provided, with colored pencils and markers, and teens can make their own greeting cards to be sent to local nursing homes or sent to soldiers stationed abroad. This is a way to give volunteers creative work that still makes a difference and doing it in library spaces just makes the library seem that more connected to the community. Prompts can be changed seasonally or teens can feel free to make their own designs and greetings on blank cards.

There are many organizations that help homemade cards get sent to soldiers overseas. Research and see what best fits the library's mission and community.

- A Million Thanks: http://amillionthanks.org/send_a_letter.php[1]
- Military-Missions.org: https://military-missions.org/care-packages/cards/[2]
- Operation Gratitude: https://www.operationgratitude.com/express-your -thanks/write-letters/[3]
- Operation We Are Here: http://www.operationwearehere.com/Ideasfor SoldiersCardsLetters.html[4]
- Soldiers' Angels: https://soldiersangels.org/cards-plus-team.html[5]

Teens can also make mini book displays about books they are reading for school. Have them find their required reading books and write a brief summary or review of the book on an index card. Showcase the books at the end of an aisle in the Young Adult or Classics section, or on a separate display area near the front of the library, if space is

Figure 5.2. Holiday greeting cards created by teens at a Memphis library and donated to a local assisted living home.

available. If librarians are responsible for creating displays, this will help them mark a task off their list thanks to the help of volunteers. Other students might be looking for these same books to read for school, so it might save librarians a bit of time when patrons can get the book from the display instead of asking for it to be found on the shelf. It also helps teens to connect what they are learning in school with the world outside of school. They might enjoy sharing their thoughts on a book in a way that is not graded; their review or summary is not a test or a report, and they do not have to love the book, they can just share how they felt about reading it.

FreeRice.com is a site that allows people to play trivia games, and each correct answer donates ten grains of rice to the World Food Programme to help end hunger.[6] This could be an activity teen volunteers do to help reach beyond library walls. This might require a bit more monitoring, as the volunteer coordinator or a library employee might have to walk by teens to make sure they are on the FreeRice.com website instead of surfing the Internet, so the library might decide it is not worth offering as a volunteer duty. The volunteer coordinator could ask that anyone who selects this task prints off a screenshot of how much rice they donated at the end of their shift, to help them stay focused and keep them accountable. The library could even create a volunteer login that keeps a running total of how much rice has been donated by all volunteers. One email address can register up to thirty-nine students, so they will be able to stay anonymous. This would be an excellent way to give teens a goal to reach and help them see how much they have helped others with their volunteer time. The volunteer coordinator could even hold FreeRice. com trivia contests and tournaments; not only will that help donate food to the hungry, but it would also create a teen program for the library and give teens another chance to earn volunteer hours. Win-win-win!

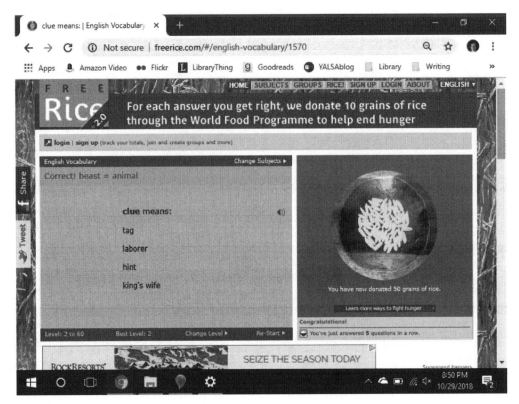

Figure 5.3. FreeRice.com is a site that allows users to play trivia games; each correct answer donates ten grains of rice to someone in need.

The standard job duties like helping with programs and cleaning books, in addition to shelving, can also be available for school year volunteers. Keep in mind that weekend schedules might prevent the same volunteer from helping set up the program and clean up after, as they might only be available in the morning before going to a lesson or game later in the day. Being flexible about what is required to sign up for a volunteer task is key with school year student volunteers.

Orientation

It is usually best to start a school year teen program after a summer teen program has been implemented. That way, the volunteer coordinator has an idea of how teen volunteers perform and can adjust the orientation accordingly. If teens who had longer shifts in the summer were unable to complete a task, then that task needs to be further broken down for school year volunteers, so they can complete it in even smaller shifts.

If teens who volunteered during the summer are continuing their commitment through the school year, a brief orientation refresher should suffice. The volunteer coordinator can tell the teen that the same jobs are available (with the exception of the Summer Learning table, or any seasonal jobs that were only offered in summer), the same professionalism and dress code are required, the method of signing in and out is the same, but scheduling is more flexible. The teens can go ahead and get started with the jobs they have been doing all summer. If any questions come up, they can ask during a shift. If they need a refresher on training, it can be scheduled at the beginning of their next shift.

Being flexible with volunteer orientations is important for school year volunteers. Holding two or three group volunteer orientations worked in summer because a lot of teens were coming in to do the same tasks, and the same scheduling was available to all of them. With school year volunteers, a teen might only be able to help with Saturday morning programs. If at all possible, their orientation should be a brief session on a Saturday morning before the program, then jump right into the work. Once they experience the task, they can ask clarifying questions afterward. Having individualized orientations on the first day of a new volunteer's shift will give them a chance to learn their specialized task and ask questions that will help them do their work. Asking school year volunteers to come in all together at a certain time to learn about the library and possible volunteer tasks could be an inconvenience to some and might make them drop out because they cannot attend the orientation.

If the library wants to be as strict with school year volunteers as they are with summer volunteers or does not have the flexibility to provide one-on-one brief orientations, it is fine to require teens to attend one of two volunteer orientations. Offer one in the evening after school events are finished and offer one on a Saturday morning or afternoon—or both. Keep in mind that this might limit the school year volunteer pool, and that it is best to be flexible with this population at this time of year because of everything they have on their plates.

Scheduling

As with the orientation, scheduling volunteer shifts should be flexible for school year volunteers. Leave hours open after school and in the evenings for teen volunteers to come in and complete tasks. Keep weekend hours available, too. This does not mean that adult volunteers cannot come in during those times, but they should do tasks that teen volunteers are not able to do, to ensure that teens will have enough to keep them busy. This is where the card making station, book review displays, and FreeRice.com trivia will come in handy—they are teen-specific volunteer duties. Try to think up as many other teen-specific jobs that can be done anywhere in the library, so they will always have a task they can do.

Depending on how many teens are volunteering during the school year, it might be ideal to limit teen volunteers to one shift a day on weekdays. That way, only one teen is coming in to shelve Mondays after school. Whatever is not finished Monday, the Tuesday volunteer can work on, and so on through the week. Having two or more teen volunteers each afternoon might lead to more socializing than working, but the volunteer coordinator will know the teens who are signing up for shifts and can use their best judgment. If two or more teens are working each weekday shift, one can be assigned to shelve while the other cleans books, and when those tasks are done, one can design greeting cards to donate while the other writes book reviews for a new display. Giving each volunteer specific duties will help keep them on task and give them a goal to reach by the end of their shifts.

Weekends might mean the library needs more teen volunteers. Two can help with children's programming: setting up, being an extra set of hands for the craft, and cleaning up after. Two can shelve in the Young Adult section and two in the Children's section to make sure everything gets put away before the new week starts and a barrage of books come through the book drop. Weekends might be a good time to bring in volunteers to help clean up around the library, shelf read, or shift books to the front of the shelf to keep the library looking nice. This will help the library stay appealing for patrons while creating volunteer hours for teens who need them.

Consider how flexible the library will be about teens calling out from shifts during the school year. It is imperative that the volunteer coordinator is strict during the summer, with so many teens wanting service hours and committing to the library at the beginning of the summer. During the school year, however, teens might have research papers or projects assigned that they need to work on. Their team might schedule an extra practice, or they might have to travel to an away game. If they call out after school for a shift that evening, are they penalized? Does the volunteer coordinator ask for a reason and rank the absence based on the excuse? This depends on the volunteer coordinator and the library administration but should be decided before any school year volunteers are hired. After all, school year volunteers are still making a commitment to the library, just as summer volunteers did.

Accountability and Rewards

The accountability and rewards for teens volunteering during the school year will be very similar to teens volunteering in the summer, with a few exceptions. Since teens are juggling their volunteer duties on top of schoolwork and extracurricular activities, the threshold for volunteer hours will be decreased. This means a teen might be rewarded for five hours of volunteer time during the school year, whereas in summer there was no reward until they hit ten hours of work. Letters of recommendation should still be offered, since this is a major incentive to volunteer. With school year volunteers having different tasks, like designing and donating cards and making book displays, they can have more freedom to create their own volunteer duties once they hit certain goals of volunteer hours.

Ensure that teens are signing in and out for each shift. They are still to make sure they are on time and being responsible for marking that time. If breaks are permitted, which might only be necessary during longer weekend shifts, teens should sign in and out for breaks also. A teen forgetting to sign in should not mean that they do not get credit for their shift because they are learning about the work environment through this experience, but make sure a great importance is put on the act of signing in and out on time. Once the habit is instilled with the first few shifts, it will be mindless, and teens will do it without thinking.

Checking in with teen volunteers is important for school year volunteers because the coordinator needs to know that volunteers feel useful, valued, and not overwhelmed by their time at the library. If volunteer duties are stressing teens out too much, they might stop coming to volunteer, or they might express their displeasure to others and make the library look bad. Being flexible with their duties to lighten their load and decrease their stress levels will show them that the library cares about them, and this will influence their devotion to the library. Notes should be made on each volunteer when the coordinator checks in with them, so the volunteer tasks can be lessened the next time a specific teen comes in.

Notes should also be kept about ideas the volunteers bring to the volunteer coordinator about improving the library. School year teen volunteers might have ideas on what other tasks could be offered, like a Homework Help time that helps students learn research skills, or even to just get teens into the library to work together and have other teens to use as a sounding board. Give ideas like this a try for a few sessions, because it might take time for the program to catch on, but it might help bring more teens into the library overall. These teens might come only for the program, but they might get library cards and become regular patrons, or they might even start volunteering! Allowing teen volunteers to suggest program ideas like study sessions will empower volunteers to think more creatively and see how they can help change the library.

School Library

Having teens volunteer in the school library allows them to take ownership of the space. School administration and the school librarian might have certain ideas of what the students need in a library or media center, but students use this space every day—or do not use it at all. Getting teens into the library by offering volunteer positions will encourage them to give their input about the library or media center as a whole, and they can make it a place where students want to be, and where they will get what they need.

Simple applications can be created for school volunteers but getting recommendations from teachers and administration is a great way to easily recruit quality volunteers. Teachers can give input on students' grades and how they act in class, and this can give the librarian a general idea of how the student will be as a volunteer. Administration can check student records to see if they are involved in a lot of extracurriculars that might interfere with volunteering, and also give the librarian a heads-up if the student might need extra help or accommodations.

Administration can also recommend when students can volunteer. Is it okay for students to give up study hall time to volunteer? Can they come in early or stay late? Can "Library Volunteers" be a club that meets during school time? Find out and have a space on the application for students to mark when they would like to volunteer. Some students might not want to give up their study hall or might not be able to stay late. Knowing this on the front end will help the librarian interview and hire quality volunteers who can commit to the library.

Job Duties

School libraries will have different job duties than public libraries, because the audience is more limited. Instead of anyone from the general public using the library, only students, typically middle and high school students for teen volunteers, will be using the library.

What do students use the library for? Some schools have language arts teachers use the library during the first month of school to show students what is available, and then it is rarely used until graduation. Some schools keep computers and printers in the library, so students are always bustling in and out to complete and print their work. Regardless of what the school library is used for, there will be plenty of jobs for teen volunteers to do.

Shelving is always an important job for the library, and teaching students how different classification systems work can be a nice lesson in addition to counting as a volunteer orientation. Student volunteers can help their peers with computer and printer use inside the library. Many high school librarians also manage various technological duties around the school; library volunteers could also help with this, depending on their skill levels. It is always a relief to have someone to help fix malfunctioning SmartBoards or glitchy PowerPoint slides without having to leave the library. Some school librarians are also responsible for textbooks and teacher resources; volunteers could help in this area by cataloging and delivering books to classrooms. If the library is the main copy center for the school, students could help teachers make copies and bring their papers back to them. For any (non-confidential) task the school librarian must do, there will be a way for a volunteer to help.

Write up job duties concisely; these descriptions would ideally fit on one page, though it will depend on how many jobs are offered. Think of the paperwork a student sees every day—their volunteer time should not amount to another pile of paper to carry around or excessive information to remember. Offer students copies of the job duties if they would like to keep them to learn on their own time but put a few laminated copies near the volunteer sign-in sheet so students can sign in, pick a job, and read over the description to refresh their memory with what needs to be done to complete the task.

The overall goal should be to get teens into the library and make it relevant and interesting to them. Volunteering in the library should not be seen as a negative or a punishment, but instead it should be a privilege that students strive to earn. Empowering students to be a vital part of the school library will make this happen.

Orientation

Teachers often bring their classes, especially freshmen, to the library within the first few months of school to give them an overview of the resources they can use for research. School librarians can promote the volunteer program at this point, to get students interested when they're new to the school and might be looking for ways to get involved and feel comfortable in a new place. This initial visit can be a callback in the volunteer orientation, to have student volunteers remember their first time in the library, what they thought of it, and what they remember from that visit. Sharing these tidbits aloud can be an icebreaker for the orientation. What students do or do not remember is not the point; that class visit might be the only time they have been to the library! The point is to open a dialogue about the library, understand how students see it, and try to figure out how to make it everything they need.

A library tour fits perfectly at this point, because it will refresh students' memories of the library, or introduce them to how the library is laid out. Explain what each section is when the tour stops there and give a brief overview of how it is arranged. For example, "This is the reference section. The books are factual and include dictionaries and encyclopedias. They are arranged by Dewey Decimal number, which is a classification system that assigns a number to books based on their subject. Our reference section also includes all of the school's yearbooks, from 1975 to now, arranged chronologically." There will be time later to teach students details about how the Dewey Decimal System works, and they can be tested with online games, worksheets, or arranging books on a cart to be checked over before shelving. Tell them where returned books can be found and sorted, and where they can park book carts when sorting and shelving books. Student volunteers will be a great help to the library, but it is important to make sure they do not take up an entire aisle while shelving; other students will still need to get around the library while volunteers are working.

If duties besides shelving are available for volunteers, show students the relevant areas. If they can help classmates with computer work and printing papers, take them to that section and explain some basic troubleshooting that comes up frequently in the library.

Teens will probably have firsthand experiences with these problems, and the knowledge to fix them. It is still a good idea to go over common issues, so they know what to expect. Make sure to tell volunteers if there are any areas they cannot be in, like the librarian's office, or any place where confidential student or school information is kept.

Show volunteers where the sign-in sheet is kept, and make sure they know the importance of signing in for each shift. If they are volunteering during the school day, signing in at the library may be the only way to verify that they are not skipping class! If students are volunteering after school, it is important to have record of their whereabouts so they will be easy to find for dismissal, or if something comes up regarding attendance or the time they left school. This is also an easy way to keep track of volunteer shifts in case of service hours earned or volunteer awards given at a school presentation. Make sure they know the job duty description page will always be with or near the sign-in sheet, so they can clock in and prep themselves for the work at the same time.

Scheduling

Decide how to schedule volunteers based on how the school administration views volunteers. If it counts as a club, volunteers can come in during club time to work. Some schools allow clubs to meet during school hours, and some are after-school only. Either can work for the library. If student volunteers can come in during study halls, make sure they are making a practical commitment to volunteering, and keeping a balance with their school and personal life. Students do not need to give up every study hall to volunteer, but they should commit to several shifts a month. Checking with teachers for information on students might help pick and schedule volunteers.

In a school setting, volunteer hours do not actually need to be documented as full hours each shift; it might work better to use a half-hour or even fifteen-minute schedule. Class periods are forty-five to fifty-five minutes long, or up to ninety minutes for schools on the block schedule. Breaking volunteer time into smaller increments allows for more accurate time keeping. It will also empower students to come volunteer as they have time, instead of feeling discouraged that they do not have a full hour to donate to the library. Breaking schedules into smaller blocks of time might also help students find the right balance between school work and volunteer work. For example, a student can use their study hall time to finish homework, then come volunteer in the library for the last thirty minutes of class.

Scheduling in a school library might also require a cap on volunteer time. It is important to keep students from feeling pressured to volunteer as much as possible. While getting more volunteer time dedicated to the library will benefit the library, the librarian, and the students, it is crucial that students know their help is above and beyond, and that the library will still be available even if they cannot dedicate a lot of time to it. Having students volunteer no more than once a week, depending on the school administration and the other commitments a student has, might be a good cap on volunteer time. It will allow students to come in frequently enough to feel like they are helping the library, without stressing them out and adding a lot to their workload.

Accountability and Rewards

Having a sign-in sheet for student volunteers will keep them accountable. Instead of a general spreadsheet with the date, their name, the time in, and the time out, it might be best to have a sheet for each student volunteer. These sheets can be monthly, quarterly, or by semester. It will allow the student to see how much time they have been donating to the library, as well as keep students from seeing who has signed in recently, and for how long. While volunteering can be a group project, especially if the librarian encourages students to work as teams, comparing volunteer time and commitment does not need to be discussed. Teens should only be concerned with their own hours and commitment, so having their personal page for signing in and out might help head off this issue.

Table 5.3. Individual sign-in sheets for student volunteers gives the teens a sense of privacy and keeps them from comparing hours with others.

STUDENT'S NAME _____

DATE	TIME IN	TIME OUT	TOTAL TIME WORKED

Planning a rewards system before launching the program is a good way to let students know what they can qualify for and what they will earn by committing to the library.

Students who are volunteering for service hours, honor societies, or community clubs will feel rewarded by the hours they earn. Some students, however, are volunteering just to be active in the school, or to help in the library, or to fulfill their school club requirement. They might appreciate a different acknowledgment of their service. Offering letters of recommendation to all students is a good way to inspire them to be hard workers. The school librarian can write letters recommending students for other volunteer positions, future jobs, honors classes at school, or even letters for college applications. It is a good idea to mention this to students when they start to volunteer, or even in the announcement that the library is looking for volunteers Students often do not think about what they might need letters of recommendation for until it is time to submit said letters. Putting this out up front will have them thinking about what they need letters for and how they can earn them, and volunteering at the library will look like a good option for them.

Students with perfect attendance who never miss a volunteer shift might earn a higher volunteer title within the library's volunteer program, or they might be presented with a certificate at the end of the semester or school year. Maybe every student who volunteers will get a certificate because they donated time to the library, while outstanding volunteers earn a gold certificate, or are named on the announcements or during an honors program. This depends on the librarian's preference, how the volunteers performed overall, and how the school distributes honors and awards.

The volunteer titles, however, can be done entirely within the library. All students start as volunteers, but after a student shows initiative, brings good ideas and practices to the library, and does not miss a shift, they might be eligible to be a senior volunteer. They can help oversee new volunteers, or lead library tours for volunteer orientations, or even assist with classes that come into the library. Empowering the students with added responsibility will pay off within the volunteer program and will be reflected in other areas of the student's schoolwork.

Letting shelvers pick a book to highlight by writing a short review for a "Staff Picks" type of a display could be a nice perk. Students will feel valued by the library and will be able to reach classmates on a different level. Similarly, marking shelves as "Adopted by [volunteer's name]" will show students and faculty who use the library that someone is putting books away and maintaining the shelves in a certain area.

If students are scheduled to volunteer but do not show up for their shift, librarians should check with the attendance office. If the student is absent, the shift can be excused, or the student can be allowed to make it up after they come back to school. If the student is not absent, the librarian might need to check with the homeroom or study hall teacher to see why the student has not showed up for their volunteer shift. Depending on the school administration and commitment to the volunteer program, it might be possible to get a list of absent students emailed every morning, so the librarian can amend the volunteer schedule at the beginning of the day. It might also be an option to have the homeroom or study hall teacher send an email after attendance is taken in class. Checking up on absent students like this might be more work for the librarian, but it is important to make sure that students are not signing up for volunteer shifts and then skipping school. Conversely, the librarian might not want to check up on students at all, and simply turn in a list of students who missed volunteer shifts to the attendance office at the end of the day. If a student has skipped their shift, that is on them. This is something that will vary according to the librarian's and school administration's outlook on truancy and how students should be responsible for their actions.

Students who missed volunteer shifts due to excused absences can be handled according to the librarian's discretion. Since a school absence affects the student's school records, should it also affect their volunteer hours? Should they be allowed to make it up the next day they are back at school? If they can make up missed shifts, will the initial absence still be reflected in their recognition at the end of the year, or in their recommendation letters?

Children Volunteers

Children volunteers are those up to age eleven, but the age for the youngest volunteers will depend on what works best for the library. Children volunteers usually start at about seven but allowing adult volunteers to bring along younger children might be an ideal way for kids to see how volunteer work is done and how it benefits everyone.

Having a volunteer program that children can participate in might seem like a disaster waiting to happen, like trying to herd cats. In reality, giving children the responsibilities of a volunteer position empowers them to act maturely and greatly contribute to the library and the community at large. This does not mean that children need to be taught how to shelve books, or even work on the library floor, but it does open the volunteer program to a new population that can benefit the library.

Summer Volunteers

Summer is always a great time to launch a new volunteer program, because time is more flexible for most parties involved, and there is more to be done around the library. This can conversely make it a little tough to launch a volunteer program, since library staff will be pulled in countless different directions. Building the program in the spring means it will run smoothly once summer begins, but keep in mind there are always hiccups down the road!

Job Duties

Children volunteers are typically too young to shelve; it is not that it cannot be done, but more that they are willing and able to easily do other tasks that will help the library.

- Children can help arrange supplies used in baby storytimes or children's programs.
- They can prepare craft supplies for programs.
- They can help set up for programs for these age groups and help clean up afterward.
- Children can help arrange materials in the children's section, like straightening books on the shelves, righting fallen display books, and picking up any early literacy materials that are included in that section.
- Children can recommend books to other young patrons. This is a fun and engaging job duty, because the volunteers can interact with peers and possibly meet new friends. If a volunteer is too shy to do this, it is perfectly acceptable for them to choose another task. If a volunteer is found to talk too much to patrons, they can be pulled temporarily from the job. They can be told to limit their conversation but remember that chatty children are hard to curb sometimes! Make sure any feedback given to children is positive and productive so they are reassured that they are doing a good job, but can learn from the volunteer coordinator's input.

Just as the teens had a greeting card volunteer station, children can have a similar set up. They can design and write cards to local nursing homes, soldiers overseas, or children receiving treatment at local hospitals.

Several organizations will help children volunteers send their cards to young hospital patients.

- Cards for Hospitalized Kids: http://www.cardsforhospitalizedkids.com/[7]
- Doing Good Together: https://www.doinggoodtogether.org/bhf/create-greeting-cards/[8]
- I See Me! Letters of Love: https://www.iseeme.com/en-us/letters-of-love.html[9]
- Nationwide Children's: https://www.nationwidechildrens.org/greeting-card[10]
- Send a Smile 4 Kids: https://sendasmile4kids.blogspot.com/[11]

Think beyond greeting cards and see if children can craft decorations to decorate the walls of children's hospital rooms. Can they create short comics, books, flip books, or graphic novels to donate to these children? Depending on the hospital and how precarious the patient's health is, some items might not be allowed in the room. See if the decorations and books could be kept in the waiting room instead, to help raise the spirits of visiting families and siblings.

Since 2015, Cedar Mills Community Libraries in Portland, Oregon, has held a Read for Goats challenge. For just over a month each winter, the libraries ask the community to log its reading hours. If they read six thousand or more hours, the libraries donate a pair of goats to a family in need living in a rural area. The family then uses the goats to start their own herd, drink and sell the milk, and more. It is a nice benefit to the family in need that will give them a helping hand. Readers in the community who might not read for a prize incentive might feel compelled to read to help others in such a meaningful way.[12]

Some libraries incorporate a service component into reading challenges. Children can keep reading logs of time they read independently and with family, and if the library reaches a certain goal, they can donate supplies or funds to people and charities in need.

Reading challenges can be specific to each library's community, so the readers participating can see the results of their efforts. It might also be a good idea to get the community involved by voting from a small selection of charitable causes, so they feel more compelled to participate in something they care about.

If the library uses a reading challenge as a volunteer opportunity, remind children that reading hours count when the child is reading independently, when they are listening to their parents or teacher read aloud, and even when listening to audiobooks. Knowing there are not really limits to the definition of "reading" will empower children to become wide readers and jump into the project with gusto.

Consider spreading the word of the reading challenge to local schools of all levels. The teachers and librarians who read aloud to students can keep a class log to turn in to the library. This is a great way to get library outreach in a fun, easy way—the schools will be partnering with the public library, but there will not be much extra work on behalf of either entity, so both parties will benefit. The public library will be affiliated with the school, possibly get some new patrons interested, and earn more reading hours for the challenge. The school will be working with an outside entity in the community, promoting literacy, and helping those in need.

Orientation

Holding small group orientations for children seems to be best practice, because they see that they are not the only children volunteering and feel proud of being part of a team. Children can meet people beyond their scope of school, home, and smaller community. Training several children at once also lets them know that they can ask each other for help if they forget a step or think they are doing a task incorrectly. A small group of children also might be more vocal during the orientation, meaning instead of hearing silence after asking "Are there any questions?", a few children might actually speak up and ask questions that will benefit the group.

Encourage parents to stay for orientation if they are interested, or if it would make them or the children more comfortable. It is better to allow parents to see what their children will be doing, and for children to see their parents nearby, at the beginning of their commitment, instead of having parents shadow their children the whole time they are volunteering, or even doing some of the work for their children. Parents staying during the orientation may also benefit the children's volunteer program, because parents may think of chores their children do around the house and how those tasks can be applied to the library.

Scheduling

For children volunteers, a weekly hour-long shift is ideal. An hour is plenty of time to do the tasks around the children's section that need to be done, and it is unreasonable to expect to keep a child focused and busy for more than an hour. Talk with children and their parents to see what day of the week works best for their volunteer shift. Try to keep it the same day and time every week for consistency. If children would like to volunteer with a friend, it is fine to have a few volunteers working on the same task or in the same area. With a volunteer program aimed at children, the goal is less what they can accomplish for the library and more that they are feeling engaged with, valued by, and at home in the library.[13] Laying this foundation when they are young will ensure the children become lifelong library supporters and users, and possibly even long-term volunteers.

Schedules for children volunteers helping with programs might be another story. If they are helping prep for the program, will help during or attend the program, and help clean up afterward, their shift could easily last three hours. Because they will be doing different things and have the program in the middle, which feels less like "work," it is probably a good job to give to the older children volunteers. Younger volunteers who still want to help with this job might want to start by helping with prep and getting the program started or coming in halfway through the program and staying to clean up. This job duty will also most likely be once a week, for Saturday programs at the library. Programs held after school hours might be earmarked for attendance only, meaning children volunteers can come to the program, but after a long day of school they are only enjoying the program, not feeling pressured to help.

Many libraries have guidelines about when children are old enough to be left unattended. This rule might be slightly amended for children volunteers if parents do not need to stay for their entire shift. Even for the volunteers working an hour shift, parents might want to use that time for brief errands. Since the children will be doing volunteer duties and either the volunteer coordinator or a library employee can keep an eye on them, it is worth letting the parents leave as long as they pick their child up on time. Keep records of when children are dropped off and picked up for volunteer shifts. Request that parents walk in with their child volunteer and sign in with them and come in to the library to sign them out. This will save the library the liability of having a child walk out of the building alone, thinking their parent is waiting in the parking lot, and not finding them there.

If other children or their parents notice the children left unattended, make it known that these children are volunteering and contributing their time to the library, so the parents do not think they can also leave their children alone in the building. Have the children wear lanyards or badges clearly labeled "Volunteer" so their purpose is clear to others.

Table 5.4. Children volunteer sign-in sheets should have a space for parents' signatures, too, just to play it safe.

DATE	CHILD'S NAME	TIME IN	PARENT SIGNATURE	TIME OUT	PARENT SIGNATURE

Accountability and Rewards

For children volunteers, records will still be kept regarding their hours and feedback about the program, but the stakes are lower than with teen and adult volunteers. Some elementary schools may require their students to earn service hours, and this can happen at the library, but the level of engagement is most important for these volunteers, compared to how often they come and what jobs they complete.

Volunteers who never miss a shift should get special recognition. These children might get a star on their volunteer badge, or even be called "Star Volunteers" and have a special badge labeling them as such. These volunteers might get a special shift where they can bring a friend who does not come to the library, and the child gets to show their friend the tasks they do. Star volunteers might get a chance to attend a program for fun but have it count as volunteer time. Maybe they can pick a movie to check out but keep it a week beyond its due date. At this level, rewards do not have to be prizes or toys; the concept of being spotlighted is enough. Even rewarding them by knowing their names and introducing them to other patrons as a volunteer will empower them to work harder for the library. All of this positivity will come through when they talk about their experiences at the library with peers, classmates, friends, teachers, extended family, and more. It is the best kind of word of mouth the library can hope for!

School Year Volunteers

With children volunteers typically committing to one hour a week, there might not be a huge change between what is done during the summer and what is done during the school year. A few minor changes may be made, however, and the program can also grow in different directions during the school year.

Public Library

Job Duties

Visits to the public library during the school year are often made because the children need to get a book to read for school—for required reading or for a book report. Children volunteers can help pull required books for their class and put them on display so when their classmates come in for a copy of the book, they can find it immediately instead of asking the library employees. This will greatly help library staff save time, and library employees and patrons alike will know immediately if there are copies of the book available or not. The children volunteers can also make a poster for the display. If only one elementary school is local, the poster can have the book titles and authors, and what grade each is required for. If several schools share the public library, the poster can just reference required reading and list the schools nearby. A list of what grades and what schools need what book can be attached to the display, or it can be left off since students will know what books they need.

Similarly, after the required reading assignments have been turned in, children can write brief reviews of the books read to add to the display. To encourage engagement with younger patrons, a voting box can be added to the display, with slips of paper for students to circle a thumbs up or a thumbs down. The votes can be collected for a week or two, then shown in a results panel on the next book display.

Orientation

The orientation for school year children volunteers is essentially the same as for summer volunteers, since their shifts and job duties will largely remain unchanged. Having a small group of volunteers is preferable if possible to encourage socializing and asking questions that everyone needs to hear the answer to. Holding the orientation as a group might also inspire some natural group work, which might create tasks that the volunteer coordinator had not previously thought of.

Some minor changes might be made to be clear that any extra jobs that were available during the summer are not available now, but that will not apply to children volunteers as much as it does for adults and teens. An announcement should be made that more flexibility is allowed regarding calling out of shifts, since there will be more for children to juggle during the school year. A strong commitment is still requested, but the library understands about school projects, events, and family issues coming up and will work with children to reschedule volunteer shifts whenever possible.

Remember, allowing parents to stay during the orientation is fine, especially if it means everyone involved will be more comfortable with independent volunteering in the future. Some parents might have ideas on duties their children could perform or how to streamline the work. Letting parents see how orientation is led and what jobs the children will be performing might also inspire them to tell friends about the program so their children can get involved as well.

Scheduling

With children volunteer shifts averaging about an hour, it is ideal to ask parents to stick around for that time period. They can browse or sit and read but they are encouraged to volunteer at the same time as their child. They will already be at the library and even one hour of putting away books or shelf reading will help the library. Getting parents involved will make the children's volunteer program pay off immediately by potentially doubling the volunteer hours donated at one time.

Establish with library management and administration if parents can leave their children volunteers. The children will have a purpose and can be checked in on by the volunteer coordinator or other library staff, so it is different than when children are left unattended on a computer or in the stacks. If parents can leave, make sure they sign in with their children and come inside of the library to sign them out. Make sure the volunteer coordinator or another library employee are able to keep an eye on the volunteers for most of their shift, or at least check in every ten minutes or so. Children volunteers will be working in the same area, so the employee who comes by can have the sign-in sheet to check off who is supposed to be working and make sure they are all accounted for.

Accountability and Rewards

Just as during the summer volunteer program, it is important to remember that for children volunteers, the stakes are lower than with teen and adult volunteers. The level of engagement is most important for these volunteers, compared to how often they come and what jobs they complete.

If the children's schools require service hours, be sure to keep track of their hours and make notes about the work they are doing. In this case, their work might not be what they are actually doing for the library, but rather how actively they are working, how long they stay focused and on what tasks, how they interact with others, and more. Developing these skills at such a young age will tell a lot about young volunteers and their personality and potential. Keeping this in mind, writing a letter of praise to the students' teachers and principal might be a nice reward. The library can periodically offer certificates of gratitude to the volunteers but making sure they get acknowledgment from other communities they are established in will help them feel proud of their accomplishments and want to give back more, in different ways. By spreading the word about what children volunteers are doing, the library is empowering volunteers and showing that it is a good place to donate time and that volunteers are valued there. If the volunteer coordinator or other library employees can visit the school during an honors program, they can even present the certificates to the star volunteers, which will get the library more into the public eye and be a very meaningful act of outreach.

School Library

Elementary students volunteering in their school library will make them feel like an important part of the school. Depending on the size of the student population and how the school schedules special classes, classes might visit the library for forty-five minutes every week or an hour every two weeks, and that might be the only chance they have to go inside the school library. Some students might not have opportunities to visit the public library, so this limited exposure to the school library might be all they get. The school librarian will certainly be providing quality resources and a curriculum that empowers students to use the library independently and pick the right books with minor guidance but bringing in students as volunteers will help the library become a major pillar of the elementary school. Having teachers recommend well-behaved students who complete their work on time is an ideal way to get the student volunteer program started on a strong note.

Job Duties

Depending on time constraints for library classes, open checkout, and volunteers in the school library, the librarian might have to get creative with job duties. Some might come from how teachers keep students in check when behavior runs rampant: "Come sit with me." Look at the duties the librarian does in the school library and see what can easily be handed over to student volunteers. Larger tasks might be broken into smaller steps that can be adapted for volunteer assistance.

Student volunteers can wait at the circulation desk while their classmates return their books, then neatly stack the books with barcodes facing up so the librarian can easily check books back in after the lesson. This task can come with some added responsibility if students prove themselves to be good volunteers: eventually they can scan the books in on their own! What student does not love to use the scanner? Not to mention how important and responsible it makes them seem to classmates. Let student volunteers know that there is room for growth within their job duties and see how they behave accordingly. Students love getting some freedom and responsibility, so it is worth telling them up front what can come to them if their work is high quality.

Student volunteers can also take turns holding the book the librarian is reading to the class. If the librarian prefers to hold it, then a student volunteer can turn the pages. Not only does this mean they will have to focus on the story so they know the right time to turn the page, but they will also be an example for their classmates, standing in front of the group and doing an important task that impacts everyone in the library.

If the class's teacher has asked for books to be pulled for future lessons, a student volunteer can be responsible for taking these books back to the classroom for the teacher. If other teachers have requested books, a model student volunteer could use the library hall pass and deliver these books after the lesson has ended. One student volunteer might even be assigned to carry the class's books back to the room.

Older student volunteers can help shelve books, especially fiction books that are organized alphabetically. After they show that they know how to do the task, they can try their hand at shelving in the nonfiction section. Student shelvers can also be spotlighted by "adopting" a few shelves in the library. This means a nice certificate will be put up naming them responsible for the shelves, and they can come in, look for returned books that need to be shelved there, and do the work. They are also responsible for keeping the shelf looking nice and keeping it in order even when there are no new books to shelve. If the volunteers do a good job with this task, they can be further applauded by having a chance to book talk a book from their shelves. A book talk shares the highlights of a book to convince others to read it, similar to a movie trailer. This will draw their classmates' attention to the fact that the student volunteer has responsibilities that earn them special privileges.

Orientation

Elementary students typically spend the first library class or two learning about the layout of the library, how things are shelved in the library, how to act in the library, and what they can do in the library. These might be very generalized lessons initially; for example: "Picture books are on the left side of the checkout desk, chapter books are on the right side of the checkout desk. Books in both of these sections are shelved alphabetically by author's last name. Informational or nonfiction books are on the shelves along the walls. They are arranged by a number relating to their subject matter in a system called the Dewey Decimal System. We will learn around this later. In the library, we walk, we do not run. We talk quietly, in whispers, or not at all. We raise our hands to ask questions or ask for help. We come to the library to share a story, learn a lesson, and check out a book to take home."

General information like this is a good foundation for the student volunteer orientation. Go over this information again, and make sure students know how to act in the library. Volunteering is a privilege, and as students have been recommended by teachers, they are most likely students who behave well and follow the rules.

Once students seem comfortable with the rules, ask them questions about where things would be found in the library. Making this a trivia game will make it more enjoyable for the volunteers and might help the information stick in their minds. Hold up sample books and see if they can determine whether it is a picture book or a chapter book, fiction or nonfiction. Give them three fiction books and see if they can arrange them in alphabetical order. Count this orientation and training time as volunteer hours so students realize it is important for them to learn everything and do it correctly. Always give time for students to ask questions and try a task independently.

Worksheets are often seen as either the best thing or worst thing a teacher or librarian can do, but there are great options for alphabetization worksheets for elementary students, and some can be found or easily created that relate directly to library shelving. Have student volunteers complete worksheets that can be kept in their files and shown to teachers and administration who want to see proof of what volunteers are doing in the library. Once volunteers get settled in and comfortable with their tasks, the librarian can invite teachers and administration to observe volunteers while they are working.

Scheduling

Making time for volunteer duties can be difficult in an elementary school, since so much time is marked for the various subjects and specials classes. Students have a short time for lunch and need to eat since they are growing; they also need recess for the same reason. The best solution is to have teachers recommend students who are at the top of their class, finish work quickly, and need a task to do beyond additional worksheets. Sending out a memo asking for a few recommended students from each grade is a great way to start the in-school elementary volunteer program.

Due to working parents, a lot of schools offer before and after care, often extending the school's hours from six in the morning to six at night. The school librarian can agree to come in early a morning or two a week, or stay late an evening or two, and oversee the volunteers until they get settled. Once volunteers understand their tasks, they could easily complete them with little oversight, meaning the employee watching the after care group that is in the library could be supervision enough. Make sure this is acceptable with school administration before starting the program. Knowing that student volunteers are recommended by teachers should be enough for administration to give the program at least provisionary approval.

While volunteers are learning their tasks, the librarian can write observations that show how independent the volunteers are becoming. The librarian can step back over time and see how the volunteers act when they do not think anyone is watching them. Any notes about these behaviors can be used to push for the volunteer program being given more time during the school day, and the volunteers getting more independence in their tasks.

Depending on how the librarian structures library lessons, there might be time in class for volunteers to help. If books are returned at the beginning of class, volunteers can stack them while everyone gets settled for the lesson. After the lesson, as students take turns browsing for books and checking them out, volunteers could shelve the books that were returned by the previous class and have already been checked in. They can help stack paper for the next class to use for notes or gather pencils for each table. Volunteers can also help clean up after their classmates, though in an ideal situation everyone would pick up after themselves. Volunteers can collect pencils and completed papers from their classmates so they are not left behind at the end of class. Since there is usually not much time between classes, every little bit of help will benefit the librarian.

Accountability and Rewards

Since student volunteers are getting the job by being recommended by teachers, they are already recognized as good students. This does not mean that the librarian should shy away from giving certificates during honors programs; bringing attention to the volunteer program will ensure that more students will want to take part in it.

As mentioned in the job duties section, students can "adopt" their own shelves, which will be marked with their names and be solely their responsibility. They can choose books to display on these shelves and can get a chance to book talk a volume from their shelves in front of the class. This will shine a positive spotlight on student volunteers, and more children might strive to be recommended as a volunteer.

Students who volunteer consistently throughout the year should be "promoted" as a volunteer for the next school year. The more seniority a volunteer earns, the more privileges they should get. This might mean they are able to earn volunteer hours by creating greeting cards to donate to nursing homes or children's hospitals, which might be seen as a more "fun" task, even though it is still an act of volunteerism.

⊚ Key Points

- Creating volunteer programs for adults, teens, and children seems like a lot to take on at once, but there is some overlap between programs. Once one is structured, it is also easier to build the others in that example.
- With the background of each volunteer program structured, there is room for volunteers to take ownership of the tasks.
- The interview and hiring process can be a chance for all potential volunteers to get experience that will help them grow on the job.
- Scheduling volunteer shifts should be flexible in most situations, with exceptions made for teens volunteering in a structured summer program.
- While job duties are written out in great detail, and need to be done to make sure the library runs smoothly, there is time for teen and children volunteers to work on cards or art that will reach beyond library walls.
- Students volunteering in school libraries will need a more structured volunteer program than those in a public library, because time constraints will be more pressing, and school administration might have a heavier hand in creating and maintaining the volunteer program.
- Letters of recommendation should be offered to volunteers of all ages and at all levels.
- Volunteers who are heavily invested in the library and the volunteer program should be given a chance to grow within the library, whether this is through promotions, special privileges, or being able to develop their own jobs and programs.

◎ Notes

1. "Send a Letter." A Million Thanks–Send a Letter. Accessed July 10, 2018. http://amillion thanks.org/send_a_letter.php.
2. "CARDS." Military Missions—Supporting Active Military and Veterans. Accessed July 10, 2018. https://military-missions.org/care-packages/cards/.
3. "Write Letters." Operation Gratitude. Accessed July 10, 2018. https://www.operation gratitude.com/express-your-thanks/write-letters/.
4. Cards and Letters for Military. Accessed July 10, 2018. http://www.operationwearehere .com/IdeasforSoldiersCardsLetters.html.
5. "Cards Plus Team." Soldiers' Angels—Cards Plus Team. Accessed July 10, 2018. https:// soldiersangels.org/cards-plus-team.html.
6. "Play Online, Learn Online and Feed the Hungry." Freerice.com | Not Your Average Online Trivia Game. Accessed September 3, 2018. http://freerice.com/.
7. "Cards for Hospitalized Kids." Cards for Hospitalized Kids. Accessed July 10, 2018. http:// www.cardsforhospitalizedkids.com/.
8. "Create Greeting Cards." Doing Good Together™. Accessed July 10, 2018. https://www .doinggoodtogether.org/bhf/create-greeting-cards/.
9. "Personalized Children's Books." Letters of Love. Accessed July 10, 2018. https://www .iseeme.com/en-us/letters-of-love.html.
10. "Send a Greeting Card." Nationwide Children's Hospital. Accessed July 10, 2018. https:// www.nationwidechildrens.org/greeting-card.
11. Hasheck, Karen. "Send A Smile 4 Kids." Send A Smile 4 Kids. Accessed July 10, 2018. https://sendasmile4kids.blogspot.com/.
12. "Read for Goats Winter Reading Challenge." Cedar Mill & Bethany Community Libraries. December 19, 2017. Accessed September 3, 2018. https://library.cedarmill.org/kids/read-for -goats-winter-reading-challenge-for-kids/.
13. Johnson, Abby. "Helping Hands: Libraries Connect Kids with Volunteer Opportunities." *American Libraries*, May 2018, 56.

◎ References

"CARDS." Military Missions—Supporting Active Military and Veterans. Accessed July 10, 2018. https://military-missions.org/care-packages/cards/.

Cards and Letters for Military. Accessed July 10, 2018. http://www.operationwearehere.com/ IdeasforSoldiersCardsLetters.html.

"Cards for Hospitalized Kids." Cards for Hospitalized Kids. Accessed July 10, 2018. http://www .cardsforhospitalizedkids.com/.

"Cards Plus Team." Soldiers' Angels—Cards Plus Team. Accessed July 10, 2018. https://soldiers angels.org/cards-plus-team.html.

"Create Greeting Cards." Doing Good Together™. Accessed July 10, 2018. https://www.doing goodtogether.org/bhf/create-greeting-cards/.

Hasheck, Karen. "Send A Smile 4 Kids." Send A Smile 4 Kids. Accessed July 10, 2018. https:// sendasmile4kids.blogspot.com/.

Johnson, Abby. "Helping Hands: Libraries Connect Kids with Volunteer Opportunities." *American Libraries*, May 2018, 56.

"Personalized Children's Books." Letters of Love. Accessed July 10, 2018. https://www.iseeme .com/en-us/letters-of-love.html.

"Play Online, Learn Online and Feed the Hungry." Freerice.com | Not Your Average Online Trivia Game. Accessed September 3, 2018. http://freerice.com/.

"Read for Goats Winter Reading Challenge." Cedar Mill & Bethany Community Libraries. December 19, 2017. Accessed September 3, 2018. https://library.cedarmill.org/kids/read-for -goats-winter-reading-challenge-for-kids/.

"Send a Greeting Card." Nationwide Children's Hospital. Accessed July 10, 2018. https://www .nationwidechildrens.org/greeting-card.

"Send a Letter." A Million Thanks—Send a Letter. Accessed July 10, 2018. http://amillionthanks .org/send_a_letter.php.

"Write Letters." Operation Gratitude. Accessed July 10, 2018. https://www.operationgratitude .com/express-your-thanks/write-letters/.

Growing and Expanding the Program

ⓖ The Value of Volunteers

DR. SARAH PETSCHONEK has always valued volunteering, to the point where she created her own nonprofit to help others in Memphis, Tennessee, easily find volunteer opportunities in their city. Dr. Petschonek works with organizations and volunteer coordinators on the front end to set up the smoothest process for volunteers to get in and out and do the most good. Without the hassle of scouting an organization, scheduling a shift, and coming in for an orientation, volunteers are free to give more productive time to an organization. As a volunteer as well as a master volunteer coordinator, Dr. Petschonek has thoughts on the value of volunteers and how to maximize the time and skills on both sides of the volunteer program.

AN INTERVIEW WITH DR. SARAH PETSCHONEK, FOUNDER OF VOLUNTEER ODYSSEY[1]

Q: **How do you define volunteering?**

SP: As librarians know, there is so much power and depth in a word. I love the word "volunteer" because it is both a noun and a verb. I think of a volunteer (n.) as someone who serves freely for the sake of doing good in our world. To volunteer (v.) is giving of one's time, talent, and energy for the greater good.

Q: **What does volunteering mean to you?**

SP: To me, volunteering is something that makes you light up. It's an act of service where you feel inspired to give your time. The real power of volunteering comes when we move away from "transactional" volunteering and embrace the idea of "transformative" volunteering.

Q: **Who benefits from volunteering?**

SP: Volunteering has a ripple effect and ultimately has the power to benefit everyone. It benefits the people we serve, the volunteer, and the community as a whole. An engaged and enthusiastic volunteer makes a huge ripple—creating a positive effect on everything and everyone around it.

Q: **What organizations should have a volunteer program?**

SP: Picture any charitable organization. Imagine walking into that organization with a magic wand that has the power to make someone appear. Any skill, talent, or ability that they need would instantly arrive in the form of a person who's willing to lend their time. If that magic wand would be welcome, then that organization would benefit from having a volunteer program.

Q: **What qualities do you think make people good volunteers?**

SP: In the right environment, anyone who willingly gives of his/her time can be an amazing volunteer. It's worth noting that not all volunteers are willing. Many people have required service hours or are "voluntold" to be there. However, people in this category can and do make good volunteers. Often people begin serving as part of a requirement but fall in love with the mission and choose to return. Regardless of how a volunteer begins with your organization, it's those who proactively and freely give their time who are most likely to make great volunteers. People of all different backgrounds, beliefs, skills, and abilities have the power to make an incredible impact if they believe in your mission and believe that their work directly benefits your cause.

Q: **What qualities do you think make organizations good places to volunteer?**

SP: I can summarize in two points what makes an organization a great place to volunteer:

(1) The WHY.

One of the most important things you can do to create a great place to volunteer is to clearly convey the mission of your organization, explain why is it important, and show the volunteers how they help you achieve that mission.

(2) Continuous Improvement.

While there are many things on a checklist of a great volunteer program, a program must grow and evolve to be great. The organization should use the mindset of continuous improvement. Actively ask the volunteers, staff, and stakeholders for ways to improve the program, implement changes to make improvements, assess whether those changes are beneficial, communicate those improvements to the volunteers so they know their input is building a better program. Repeat. Repeat. Repeat. With this approach, the other pieces will always improve.

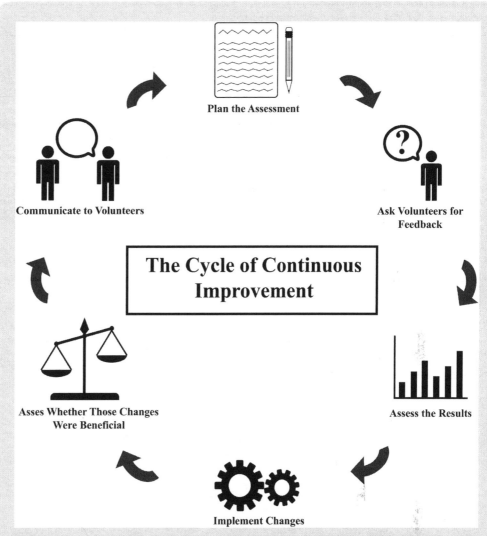

The Cycle of Continuous Improvement

Plan the Assessment

Ask Volunteers for Feedback

Assess the Results

Implement Changes

Asses Whether Those Changes Were Beneficial

Communicate to Volunteers

Figure 6.1. The cycle of continuous improvement shows how a volunteer program must grow and evolve to be great.

Q: **What most helps you match volunteers with organizations? (Coordinators, descriptions, etc.)**

SP: When we match volunteers to organizations, we look for a few key things:

(1) Clear and engaging job titles and descriptions. What skills, talents, and personalities do you need? What will they be doing? Is it tied to your mission? Is it engaging? For example, are you looking for a front desk worker to answer the phone? I'd rather see an opening for an Ambassador of First Impressions who uses their outgoing personality and love of the organization to win over callers, visitors, and guests.

(2) A clear tie to the WHY. I want an organization to convince me and to convince the volunteers that their time is being used well and benefitting a great cause. Even if the work seems tedious (reorganizing the filing cabinet), tell me that you need an organization guru to whip the files into shape so you can quick find emergency contact information.

(3) A great volunteer coordinator with a passion for the mission and a love of developing volunteers. They are the lynchpin to a successful volunteer program.

(continued)

Regular Job Title	Dynamic Job Title
Front Desk Worker A volunteer who will answer the phone for us.	**Ambassador of First Impressions** A volunteer who uses their outgoing personality and love of theorganization to win over callers, visitors, and guests.
Trash Duty Pick up trash during our event.	**Food & Beverage Ninja** Sneak through the crowd and pick up trash without being detected.
Locate Misplaced Books Put books back on the shelf.	**Book Detective** Use your detective skills to help us locate misplaced books and put them back home on their shelf.
Nursery Worker Work in our nursery room.	**Baby Hugger** Love on our adorable babies while the nursery worker changes diapers and gives medications.
Make Phone Calls Call and thank our volunteers.	**Super Hero Caller** Wow our volunteers with your thanking super powers!

Figure 6.2. Dynamic job titles get volunteers excited about the duties they will be doing. Would you rather be on Trash Duty, or be a Food and Beverage Ninja?

(4) A site visit. Within just a few minutes at a site visit, I can quickly get a sense of how the organization values its volunteers. These site visits also help me under-stand the nuances of each location so I can use informal observations to help the volunteers make the right choice. For example, is it a loud, high-energy space filled with rambunctious kids? For some volunteers, that's a bonus while for oth-ers that's a deterrent. It's helpful to have that context firsthand.

(5) Knowing the volunteer. We assess each volunteer's knowledge, skills, abilities, and personality to help match him/her with the right opportunity.

Q: What do you think are 3 key factors of a quality volunteer program?

SP: The three key factors are:

(1) A top-down belief in the value of the volunteer. Culture comes from the top. The best programs have an executive director or CEO who believes in and supports the volunteer program, a board who talks about volunteers as a valuable resource and reflects that in their strategic plan. This also includes a volunteer coordinator who "gets" it and who has the support and resources to build a great program.

(2) Continuous improvement. All roads lead back to continuous improvement. With this mindset, a volunteer program will get better and better over time.

(3) Volunteer strategy and goals. In addition to the intangible love for volunteers, a great program also needs a great strategy. As a few examples, it should include

items such as what skills are needed, plans for recruiting volunteers, and a regular system of assessing and rewarding volunteers.

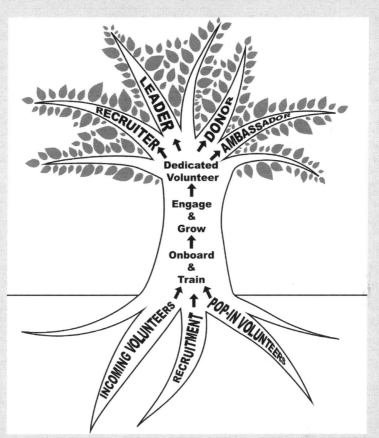

Figure 6.3. The life of a volunteer shows how volunteers can be nurtured and cared for to help expand the program in positive ways.

Q: **What inspired you to start Volunteer Odyssey?**

SP: Growing up, we often volunteered as a family, collecting food for our local food pantry. Around the time I turned seven, I started to wonder why we did this. My parents explained that there are a lot of people who work very hard, but who still need some extra help to feed their families. It might even be a kid next to me in class who would go hungry if not for the food bank. Their message was and still is this: if we can help, we should. Years later after finishing my PhD, I found myself in one of those "life is too short for this" kind of jobs. In 2012, I quit my job and embarked on my own volunteer odyssey—30 consecutive days of volunteering at 30 different organizations and writing 30 blog posts about the experience. A week in, I was completely in love with my city, and this amazing, rich world of people who dedicate their lives to service. On the flip side, I was deeply frustrated with the process of getting in the door—unresponsive organizations, difficult steps (fax machine, anyone?), and confusing directions. I became obsessed with the idea of quickly connecting people to meaningful volunteer opportunities. I wondered what I could learn from other cities, so I set off across the country, volunteering in nine different communities, so I could understand how people discover and select volunteer opportunities. After completing those two journeys, I decided to start Volunteer Odyssey. Our goal is to match everyone with their ideal volunteer opportunities and streamline that process.

Volunteer programs often get started because patrons express interest in helping out at the library, so make sure patrons know the program is coming, and give them the information about applying and scheduling. Committed patrons are a great foundation for the volunteer program, because they already know and love the library. They are part of the community and can help spread the word; since they are established in the community, other people will respect their thoughts on the library and consider joining.

Post flyers in the library and share information about the program in any print or digital newsletters the library publishes. Groups who come in to use meeting rooms and study rooms will see these flyers and be interested and help spread the word. Promote volunteer jobs at any library program or function and find potential volunteers. Talk about volunteer opportunities during teen programs to recruit students who need service hours or want to help. Share information about volunteering at the end of story time, and parents who need something to do to get out of the house might like to help. Mention it at the end of adult programs, at board meetings, and at Friends of the Library meetings.

When the volunteer coordinator or teen services librarian go on school visits, make sure they have volunteer information on flyers that will appeal to teens. Talk about the volunteer program, what jobs are available, and how the library can work with students' schedules. Invite students to ask questions or suggest jobs while library employees are in the schools. Library staff may visit their school for a library program but offering them the option of service hours will bring them into the physical library. School counselors are another valuable resource—they often help students find volunteer placements, internships, and jobs. Leaders of organizations like the beta club and honor society also need service opportunities for their members, so ask to speak to these employees as well. Let them know how many opportunities the library has to offer students and include information about group volunteering so the clubs could organize a day to come together. Often it is easier to have a whole group come, because teens will be more likely to attend. They will want to hang out with friends while they help, instead of it being up to them to come to the library, apply, and volunteer alone.

High school teachers and librarians could recommend certain students as volunteers. This could be an honor for outstanding students to be personally recommended to the library. If this happens, make sure you acknowledge that the student was picked out of the entire student body to represent the school at the library.

Present summer volunteer shifts as an internship opportunity, where students will get real life job experience, starting with the application and interview process, feedback on their work, and letters of recommendation to take with them for future job and school opportunities. There are often summer internship grants available through the Young Adult Library Services Association and other library organizations. The library can apply for these grants and have funds to pay a few teen interns. Advertise these positions as highly esteemed within the library system and mention the pay as well. Students might be battling between earning money in a summer job or earning service hours with volunteer opportunities. This grant might pull more teen volunteers into the library and help boost them and their financial needs as well.

Visit college campuses and post flyers. Speak with club leaders and department heads there. Students often need service hours to maintain scholarships. Students looking for work study might also be willing to volunteer. Work around their class schedules and offer opportunities for students to create programs based on their majors. College students have different times available for volunteering, and a different view of the world and the library system. Getting college students on board with the library will not only help the library gain more patrons from their word of mouth, but they can also give insight on how to make the library appealing to their age bracket. College students could hold "adulting" classes for the teen library patrons. They could mentor teen volunteers. They could hold programs based on starting college and getting financial aid, and the turn out might be bigger than if the same program was hosted by a library employee.

Reach out into the community and see what resources are there. Is there a community center, a gym, a YMCA, a Boys and Girls Club? These are good places to talk up the volunteer program to employees and ask to put up flyers. Parents might be interested, and employees might want to volunteer. These community centers are a great resource because not only can information be posted about the volunteer program, but also volunteer exchanges can be organized. The library and Boys and Girls Club, for example, could establish a partnership where kids attending spring break camps or summer camps could come over with employees to help clean books one day. A library employee could then trade services by coming to the community center and doing a pop-up story time with the kids, book talks, or general library promotion.

Assisted living homes might be a gold mine of volunteers. Some residents might be independent enough to go out on their own and volunteer at the library. Having a group come from assisted living could also be arranged if the organization uses bus transportation. Sign-up lists can be posted and the interested residents could come together on a day to shelve books, or maybe schedule them for a day where there is also a library program that would interest this group. They could shelve for an hour, and then attend the program. The library would be engaging with them not only as volunteers, but as patrons. Being considerate with scheduling could encourage this group to come back more often. If groups from assisted living homes came to the library, employees could create programs around them. They could read to children instead of or after story time or come read if therapy dogs visit the library. Meet with the activities coordinator at assisted living homes and see what the seniors might be interested in helping with.

Learning centers for people with disabilities are good partnerships to foster. Groups of individuals can come to the library and help clean or shelve, depending on their abilities. This is another group that is good to schedule around a program, especially a craft or read aloud program. Therapy dogs are popular, too. Forming a partnership with this group will bring new patrons into the library, and it will also show existing patrons that the library is inclusive, and all are welcome. Special education classes from area high schools are usually willing volunteers, as mentioned in a previous example. Having groups of volunteers with several teachers and assistants means the groups can be broken up and complete more tasks in one shift.

⊚ Library Outreach

Focusing on library outreach while already attempting to build a volunteer program might seem like too much to take on at once, but the two actually go hand in hand. It has been stated that volunteers are valuable members of the community, and outreach is making the library visible in the community. Having volunteers come in to the library is a wonderful first step in making the library a community-led organization, instead of just a building available for the public to come in to.

Outreach means information about the library will be accessible to the public in places people routinely visit, like farmers' markets, outdoor concerts, even at other organizations and stores. Doing regular outreach for the library will ensure it is more visible, both to current patrons and to people who might not know all the library has to offer. Outreach is also a great way to recruit more volunteers; letting people know about the library and the opportunities it offers will help them realize what skills they have to share. This means library employees are interacting with the public in public spaces, being seen, and being accessible.

The Public Library Association has a selection of outreach links available at http://www.ala.org/pla/resources/tools/community-engagement-outreach

The library having a visible presence at community events is one type of outreach, but it is an example of the library inserting itself into the community. Community-led outreach means the public is involved in deciding how the library can provide services that are accessible for everyone in the community.[2] The public takes ownership in the library and changes it, instead of the current iteration of the library popping up within the community. Both types of outreach are important and valuable and can be balanced to make the library a well-rounded community center for its population.

Community-led library outreach does not mean employees will have more work; it is just a shift in thinking and how they approach their job duties. There will be no abrupt change in how their daily work looks; rather, library staff will have some input and the community will have some input. The changes will happen over time, and everyone will need to be flexible with what is expected and how it can happen. Shifting the library to be community-led also does not mean that employees are currently doing a bad job. They are and have been doing great work, but as more resources are available online, the library as an institution needs to become exactly what each community needs. This will make libraries vary from community to community, even within the same city's system.

Instead of the library being a physical building for the public to come visit, the library should be a concept and resource for the public in the community. This means that library employees do not even have to plan all of the outreach; it should come organically from the community. Community members, whether they are library patrons or not, should all have a say in how the library as an institution benefits their community. That being said, library staff should be very involved in the process. They need to understand how the library's service being community-led will shift their duties—but not add more work.

As library employees have the insider scoop, they should consider several factors when shifting library services from being internal to being community-led. These factors include:

- Who are library users and nonusers?
- What barriers keep the public from using the library?
- What community groups can be spotlighted?
- What does it mean to be community-led? (http://publiclibrariesonline.org/2013/04/from-project-to-branch-integration-and-sustainability-community-led-work-at-halifax-public-libraries/)

Library staff need to stretch beyond their comfort levels and realize they will work with a variety of people in the community. Children's library workers who do not usually work with adults or senior citizens will have to push themselves to relate to these populations in different ways. If every library employee is comfortable enough with the entire range of the community's population, the library will immediately and easily be a more welcoming space. This is a great first step to make the library even more integral in the community.

Keep in mind that the library will always be changing. Becoming community-led does not mean there is an endpoint one year in the future. Once employees change their approach to work, they will be able to easily adapt as the community around the library changes. Young families will move in and replace the senior citizens who needed the library for meeting spaces and large print books. The young elementary school students will grow to be a large teen population hungry for library resources and programs. The community-led library will be at the center of it all.

Shifting the library to be community-led does not mean that library employees need to spend a large portion of work time out in the community. Instead, think of how many different community groups come into the library. They attend certain programs, like computer classes for seniors or conversation classes for English as a Second Language learners. They reserve the meeting room for their organizations. While library employees might have previously just counted program attendees or been hands-off with meeting room rentals, they now have a strong reason to interact with these patrons. Employees can check in with program attendees and those who rent meeting rooms to see if they are getting what they need from the library. What could make their experiences better? What could the library do to go above and beyond expectations? How can the library meet these patrons where they are in the community, instead of asking them to come into the library building? Opening conversations will establish trust with these community members and will naturally lead to them giving more feedback to the library about how the building can break down its walls.

If outreach seems like too daunting a task for the library to take on with the start of the volunteer program, look over "A Step by Step Guide to 'Turning Outward' to Your Community." This document was created by the American Library Association, in partnership with Libraries Transforming Communities, the Public Library Association, and the Harwood Institute for Public Innovation. The toolkit is a PDF that proposes a ninety-day plan for libraries to "turn outward" and put the community first. Broken into thirty-day sections, the toolkit includes questionnaires and worksheets to help the library best serve its community. See how innovative the library can be: http://www.ala.org/tools/sites/ala.org.tools/files/content/LTCGettingStarted_DigitalWorkbook_final010915.pdf

⑥ Providing Outside Opportunities

Library volunteer programs do not have to stay inside library walls. Libraries can recruit volunteers to donate their time to other organizations. Libraries can also recruit staff to volunteer with other organizations; this is another way to spread the word about the library and what it can do. Anything that gets the library into the public and into people's minds will help in some way, be it volunteer recruiting, patrons attending programs, or even circulation numbers.

The volunteer coordinator can arrange a volunteer fair to be held at the library. Offering this event on a weekend means that potential volunteers of all ages can come see what opportunities are available to help their community and city. The library can reach out to their contacts at various organizations in the city and see who needs volunteer help. The volunteer coordinator can contact outside organizations and nonprofits and connect with other volunteer coordinators. Most coordinators will gladly donate their time in exchange for a place to present their organization's mission and potentially hire more volunteers. Volunteer fairs can be held periodically, such as one in late spring, to harness summer volunteers, and one in early fall, to find new volunteers after school is back in session and when people realize they need service hours for the year.

At the volunteer fair, coordinators can set up tables of information for potential volunteers to take home. Depending on the library's community, projected program audience, and number of organizations signed up for the fair, it might be nice to have an opening session where each volunteer coordinator talks briefly about their organization's mission. This will get the word out about their organizations, so it will be worth the time they invested. It will also help potential volunteers discover who they would like to talk to for follow-up information.

A special volunteer fair can be held for incoming college students in the fall or graduating high school seniors in the spring. This fair can be more oriented to getting these young adults into the field they are interested in. Volunteer experiences at this age will greatly help students find their career path—or find out that they are not as suited to a career as they initially thought!

The volunteer coordinator can help volunteers find other opportunities beyond the library. This would be additional work but could make the library that much more valuable to the community. If there is an organization that lists volunteer opportunities, it could be as easy as the coordinator being willing to check that database for library volunteers and patrons. Once the volunteer coordinator has connections, such as after arranging a volunteer fair, they can keep a master list of volunteer opportunities to refer volunteers.

VolunteerCompass is an online database of volunteer opportunities in Memphis, Tennessee.[3] People visit the website and choose an interest or search their passion to see what volunteer opportunities are available. People can also search by date and time to see what volunteer opportunities are available, if they are looking for the time more than the interest.

This makes volunteering simple because the individual does not have to research organizations, find out if they need volunteers, and try to schedule a time on their own. All of the legwork is done for them, much like it is for the library's volunteer program, but on a larger scale.

If databases like this are not available in certain cities, research volunteer organizations to see if there is a potential partnership for the library to tap into. National organizations like Salvation Army, the Red Cross, United Way, and more usually need volunteers for set duties or special projects. It is worth having the library volunteer coordinator forge relationships with major nonprofits in the area.

⊚ Key Points

- Creating a community-led method of service will make the library even more valuable to its community.
- Rather than creating more work, shifting to a community-led library system will actually be easier on employees as they take a back seat to citizens who want to be heard.
- Volunteering does not have to stay within library walls; the library can still be a community pillar by providing outside volunteer opportunities for the community.
- Bringing outside organizations' volunteer coordinators into the library will benefit potential volunteers by giving them more options, other organizations by giving them a new audience, and the library by reinforcing the fact that it is a community institution that helps its population.

⊚ Notes

1. "Interview with Sarah Petschonek." Email interview by author. July 20, 2018.
2. "From Project to Branch Integration and Sustainability: Community-Led Work at Halifax Public Libraries." Public Libraries Online. Accessed May 9, 2018. http://publiclibraries online.org/2013/04/from-project-to-branch-integration-and-sustainability-community-led -work-at-halifax-public-libraries/.
3. GivePulse.com. "Volunteer and Make A Difference Today | Volunteer Odyssey." GivePulse. Accessed June 14, 2018. https://serve.volunteerodyssey.com/.

⊚ References

"From Project to Branch Integration and Sustainability: Community-Led Work at Halifax Public Libraries." Public Libraries Online. Accessed May 9, 2018. http://publiclibraries online.org/2013/04/from-project-to-branch-integration-and-sustainability-community-led -work-at-halifax-public-libraries/.

GivePulse.com. "Volunteer and Make A Difference Today | Volunteer Odyssey." GivePulse. Accessed June 14, 2018. https://serve.volunteerodyssey.com/.

"Interview with Sarah Petschonek." Email interview by author. July 20, 2018.

Sample Paperwork

THESE MATERIALS CAN BE ADAPTED for your organization's specific needs. Background checks may not be necessary if volunteers are not left alone with children, for example. Liability might not be a concern in certain areas. Some organizations might not want to contact or tag volunteers on social media and will not need to ask for that information. Some organizations will not use volunteers' full names on any media outlets or promotional materials, so the media release may be rewritten. All paperwork is meant to be an example and provide a jumping off point for the library's volunteer program. It is always a good idea to check with library directors, administration, boards, and any city governance that might be in the place for the library's best interests.

⊚ Volunteer Application

Printed Name _____

Previous/Maiden Name or Nicknames _____

Street _____

City _____ State _____ Zip _____

Phone _____ Email _____

May we contact you through . . .

[ ] Facebook   [ ] Twitter   [ ] Other _____ Username _____

How would you prefer we contact you? _____

Availability

[ ] Monday   [ ] Tuesday   [ ] Wednesday   [ ] Thursday   [ ] Friday

[ ] Morning   [ ] Afternoon   [ ] Evening   Specific Hours _____

I am interested in . . .   [ ] on-going volunteering   [ ] one-time volunteering   [ ] special events

Interests: What sort of work would you like to do as a volunteer? _____

_____

_____

_____

Special Skills: List any special skills, experience, or education you would bring to the organization. _____

_____

_____

_____

References: List three people, not related to you, whom we can contact for a reference.

Name _____ Relation _____ Phone _____

Name _____ Relation _____ Phone _____

Name _____ Relation _____ Phone _____

Emergency Contact

Name _____ Cell _____

Home _____ Work _____ Email _____

Street _____ City _____ State _____ Zip _____

Volunteer Liability

I, the undersigned, acknowledge that I am volunteering my time and labor to assist ORGANIZATION NAME, a nonprofit organization, in its efforts to reach its goals. My volunteer efforts may bring challenges, and I know that unanticipated or unexpected risks may be involved in any activity. I assume all risks of injury to my person and property, regardless of the nature and cause of the injury, which may be sustained in connection with my volunteer activities for ORGANIZATION NAME. I hereby, for myself, release and discharge ORGANIZATION NAME, its staff, directors, and all other volunteers, from any and all liability, claims, demands, actions and causes of action of any sort, for injury sustained to my person and/or property during my volunteer activities. I certify that my participation in this activity is voluntary, and I am not, in any way, the employee, servant or agent of ORGANIZATION NAME.

Volunteer Media Release

I also understand that photographs and/or videos may be taken of me to document my volunteerism. I give permission to ORGANIZATION NAME to use my full name, any photo/video of me and any necessary information about my volunteer work for publicity purposes.

Signature _____ Date _____

Background Check

ORGANIZATION NAME runs background checks on all ongoing volunteers and staff. These checks include searches for criminal records and verification of employment. If you intend to volunteer on a regular basis, please supply us with the additional information needed to run this check.

Date of Birth _____ Place of Birth _____ Citizen Country _____

Race _____ DL# _____ SS# _____

Gender _____ Height _____ Weight _____ Hair Color _____ Eye Color _____

I certify that the information included in this application is true to the best of my knowledge. I also grant permission for ORGANIZATION NAME to conduct a background check for the purpose of this volunteer assignment.

Signature _____ Date _____

◉ Volunteer Handbook

Definition of Volunteer

A volunteer is a person who performs a task for an organization without compensation. They are not employees of the organization but are committed to the organization's goals and help accomplish these goals by completing supplementary tasks.

Definition of Intern

An intern is a student enrolled in a higher learning program, or recently graduated from a higher learning platform, who commits to an organization for one semester or more. Interns may be compensated financially or with school credit through their institution.

About the Handbook

This handbook is intended for volunteers and interns, and for staff who work with both. It is designed to acquaint you with the organization and provide you with information about working conditions and some of the policies affecting your placement as a volunteer or intern. Please read this information carefully, as it will assist us both in keeping your experience rewarding and create a foundation for open and positive communication.

The information in the handbook is extensive; however, you will learn much of the information about specific assignments in orientation, "on the job," and by participating in available training. Any time you have questions, please feel free to contact your supervisor or the volunteer coordinator. Please keep this handbook as a reference. Once you have finished reading this guide, please sign all forms and return to the volunteer coordinator.

We know that a successful volunteer experience starts with a compatible placement, one that meets your needs and ours. The volunteer coordinator will meet with you to discuss your interests, skills, and expectations. An assignment will then be made so your goals are successfully matched with our needs. Placements are considered and discussed with each potential volunteer. Please feel free to discuss your particular needs with the volunteer coordinator.

We need volunteers of all ages, from diverse backgrounds, with varied interests to help us meet the growing needs of those in our community. Please feel free to share information regarding our volunteer opportunities with your friends and families.

Who This Handbook Covers

This handbook applies to all volunteers and interns of the organization. If organization staff asks you to do anything that violates the policies and procedures established in this document, please contact the volunteer coordinator prior to proceeding. Please take the time to review and understand this handbook. If you have any questions about this handbook, your job or any job-related issue, please feel free to ask your supervisor or the volunteer coordinator.

This handbook is not all-inclusive but is intended to provide you a summary of some of the volunteer program guidelines. This edition supersedes all previously issued editions of a handbook or guidelines.

No handbook can anticipate every circumstance or question. After reading the handbook, if you have any questions please talk with the volunteer coordinator as soon as possible. We want to know you understand the guidelines. The need may arise to change the guidelines described in the handbook. The organization reserves the right to interpret or change any guideline without prior notice.

Orientation

Orientations will be scheduled with the volunteer coordinator once the volunteer position has been officially offered to you. Some orientations will take place in a group of volunteers who will be doing similar jobs. These orientations will be offered on weekday evenings or weekend mornings or afternoons, and you will be able to attend the session that best fits with your schedule. The orientation you choose to attend has no bearing on what schedules you will be able to work at the library. In some cases, the volunteer coordinator will lead a one-on-one orientation in the case of needing a more in-depth tour and introduction to the tasks, or in the case of scheduling issues with a group orientation. Please note that one-on-one orientations are rare due to the time constraints of the volunteer coordinator. If at all possible, you should arrange to attend one of the group orientations. The sessions will be announced with at least two weeks' notice.

Orientation will include a tour of the library, explanations of what jobs will be done in what sections, and brief trainings on how each of the jobs will be completed. A more detailed training session will happen during your first volunteer shift. You will be able to ask questions during the orientation, during the training, and at any time during their volunteer commitment. The volunteer coordinator will periodically check in to make sure you feel comfortable doing your job, and you will also be able to address any questions or concerns at that time.

Training

In an effort to ensure that your volunteer experience is rewarding, we offer many opportunities for both personal and professional growth through training and meaningful work experience. As a volunteer or intern, you will be given an orientation to the organization, including information on goals, policies, services, community relationships, programming, and more. The volunteer coordinator will arrange job-specific training. In addition, you may be invited to attend staff trainings that are relevant to your assignment.

Commitment

Please live up to the responsibility of your volunteer role. Volunteer work is not something that can be done in a few odd hours when there is nothing more exciting to do. It is a commitment to others that involves a definite allotment of time, energy, preparation, and a real desire to serve. Please be present and on time for every commitment you make. If you find yourself running late or unable to meet an obligation, please call the volunteer coordinator as far in advance as possible. This will help us with scheduling extra help, if needed.

Rights and Responsibilities

As a volunteer or intern, you can expect:

- A personal interview with the volunteer coordinator from the department in which you will work.
- Appropriate training and orientation.
- A clear description of position requirements, responsibilities, and time commitment.
- A friendly, safe atmosphere in which to work.
- An open forum for communication with plenty of opportunity for feedback.
- To be treated as a valuable team member.
- A feeling of personal satisfaction.
- Interns can also expect a valuable educational experience.

The organization can expect from you:

- A time commitment. Think about how much you are able to give and discuss this with the volunteer coordinator prior to beginning an assignment.
- A willingness to participate in available training and acceptance of supervision.
- Two weeks advance notice if you need to resign.
- Respect for those you work with, staff, patrons, and the public.
- A willingness to abide by the policies included in this handbook.
- Acceptance of the organization's mission and values.

Equal Employment Opportunity

We are an equal opportunity employer and dedicated to the principles of equal employment opportunity in any term, condition, or privilege of employment. We believe every employee has the right to work in an environment that is free from all forms of unlawful discrimination. Consistent with applicable laws, we make all decisions involving any aspect of the employment relationship without regard to race, color, sex, creed, religion, age, marital status, national origin, citizenship, the presence of any sensory, mental, or physical disability, veteran status, sexual orientation, or any other status or characteristic protected by local, state, or federal law. Discrimination and/or harassment based on any of those factors are inconsistent with our philosophy of doing business and will not be tolerated. An Affirmative Action plan is on file with administration.

Our equal opportunity employment and anti-discrimination policies extend to volunteers and interns as well as employees.

Feedback for Volunteers/Interns

We are committed to recognizing your efforts through awards, day-to-day expressions of appreciation, and by treating you as a co-worker. We value your gift of time and talent. Volunteers/interns will be offered opportunities to evaluate their own services and the volunteer program.

When giving an evaluation of your volunteer time, be honest! We want everyone to enjoy their time here. If something is not working for you, tell us so we can place you with the person or activity that is the best fit. Volunteers/interns in continuous service will be reviewed by the volunteer coordinator monthly. One copy of the completed evaluation forms will be kept in the volunteer's file and one given to the volunteer, if requested.

Evaluations will include, but not be limited to the following:

- Evaluation of volunteer/intern's job performance based on the criteria listed in the position description.
- Identification of volunteer/intern's potential growth areas.
- Attainment of previously agreed upon goals, with new goals mutually agreed upon.
- Recommended training.

Evaluations required by other outside organizations—such as colleges or other referring programs—will be offered as needed.

Property and Compensation Coverage

The company will not assume any responsibility for loss, theft, or damage to personal property, including vehicles, brought to work. Anything of value should be left at home. It is recommended that volunteers/interns carry homeowner's or renter's insurance, which covers loss or theft of personal property. Volunteers/interns are not covered by or entitled to worker's compensation benefits in the event of a personal injury while performing their volunteer/intern responsibilities.

Volunteer Files

The organization maintains a file for each volunteer and intern in continuous service, which will include your original application, personal data, reference information, awards, years of service, background check, etc. This file serves several purposes including maintaining emergency contact information and a record of activities for recognition purposes. Only information that is relevant to the volunteer's or intern's activities will be kept in the file. Your personal file is confidential and is the property of the agency. Access is limited to immediate supervisor, department director, volunteer coordinator, and agency executive staff only. If you wish to review the contents of your file, please contact the volunteer coordinator.

Information contained within a volunteer's or intern's personnel file will not be disclosed to another individual or agency without the written permission of the volunteer, intern, or parent/guardian of a minor volunteer. Information related to work experience in a service area and participation in training programs may be used by the volunteer or intern for job reference purposes.

Background Check

A background check will be completed on any ongoing volunteer or intern who works directly with children and teens. You will be asked to provide additional information and sign an authorization to allow us to run the background check.

Resignation/Termination

Volunteers and interns end their relationship for a variety of reasons. The most common reason is increased personal responsibilities. Volunteers and interns are asked to submit a letter of resignation two weeks in advance if possible. Occasionally, the relationship may be terminated at the request of a staff member. Reasons may include, but are not limited to the following:

- Use of drugs and/or alcohol or being under the active influence of drugs and/or alcohol while on the job, or while representing the organization.
- Inappropriate behavior, including any physical and/or verbal abuse of staff, patrons, or others associated with the organization.
- Inconsistency in providing services.
- Non-adherence to policies and procedures as outlined in the handbook.
- Theft of the organization's property or the property of anyone associated with the organization.
- Creating an unsafe or uncomfortable work environment for others.

If necessary, a consultation with the supervisor or department director will be arranged. The final decision and course of action will be based on the person's need, volunteer program needs, and continued quality service. We hope that all of our volunteers remain with us indefinitely. Should any situation present itself, we will do our best to be fair and equitable. We understand that some situations may have extenuating circumstances. It is our intention to do the best for all involved parties.

Safety and Incident Reports

The establishment and maintenance of a safe work environment is the shared responsibility of the organization, staff, volunteers, interns, and patrons. The organization will attempt to do everything within its control to assure a safe environment and comply with federal, state, and local safety regulations. You are expected to follow agency safety rules and to exercise caution in all volunteer or intern activities. You are asked to report any unsafe conditions immediately to your supervisor.

If you feel unsafe for any reason, leave the area immediately and find a supervisory staff person. Report the situation to that supervisor and allow her to deal with it. Do not return to the area until the supervisor assures you it is safe to do so. If you still do not feel safe, return to that supervisor, another supervisor, or the volunteer coordinator and inform them you do not feel the situation has been adequately resolved to ensure your safety. You should never work in an environment where you do not feel you are safe.

All accidents that result in injury must be reported immediately to your supervisor, regardless of how insignificant the injury may seem at the time. These reports are necessary to comply with reporting regulations and to protect you in the event that future problems occur as a result of the injury. Your reports may also result in adjusting policies and procedures to prevent reoccurrences of similar threatening conditions.

All threats, accidents, and unsafe situations should also be reported to the volunteer coordinator as soon as possible. The volunteer coordinator will bring the issue to the Safety Committee, who will put a plan in place to address the situation and similar future situations.

Preventing Violence in the Workplace

The organization is committed to providing employees, volunteers, interns, and patrons with a safe work environment. Threatened or actual violence by anyone in the aforementioned groups is strictly prohibited on our premises or on a work site. Violence in the workplace may be described as verbal or physical threats, intimidation, and/or aggressive physical contact.

Prohibited conduct includes, but is not limited, to the following:

- Inflicting or threatening injury or damage to another person's life, health, well-being, family, or property.
- Possessing a firearm, explosive, or other dangerous weapon on the organization's premises or using an object as a weapon.
- Throwing objects.
- Slamming items such as doors, drawers, desks, etc.
- Damaging property belonging to the organization, employees, volunteers, or interns.
- Using obscene or abusive language or gestures in a threatening manner.

Because of the potential for misunderstanding, the organization also prohibits joking about any of the above conduct. You are encouraged to be proactive in maintaining a safe working environment by reporting violent or potentially violent behavior. If you observe or experience these types of behavior, please report them immediately to your supervisor or the volunteer coordinator. In addition, volunteers and interns working at a remote location or in the workplace of a person who experiences actual or threatened violent behavior should report it immediately to the appropriate authorities.

If you feel uncomfortable around a particular person for any reason, please report the situation to the volunteer coordinator or your immediate supervisor. These interactions may be a part of a larger pattern of behavior that might lead to an unsafe condition if not addressed quickly. If you do not feel comfortable interacting with any person, please voice your concerns to the volunteer coordinator so that a plan can be developed to prevent that person from unsupervised interaction with you.

As stated earlier in this manual, leave the area as soon as you feel it has become unsafe and report the situation to a supervisor. Do not return until you are certain it is safe to do so. The organization may choose to report any matters that endanger its employees, volunteers, interns, or patrons to law enforcement.

Duty to Warn/Report

If a volunteer or intern suspects or has knowledge that illegal or unethical behavior has occurred or is imminent, they must report the issue immediately to their supervisor or volunteer coordinator.

Use of Equipment

When using organization property, you are expected to exercise care and follow all operating instructions, safety standards, and guidelines. Please notify your supervisor if any equipment or machines appear to be damaged, defective, or in need of repair. Prompt reporting of damages, defects, and the need for repairs could prevent deterioration of equipment and possible injury to staff, volunteers, interns, or patrons.

Emergency Closings

Emergency conditions such as severe weather can disrupt agency operations and interfere with work schedules, as well as endanger a volunteer's well-being. These extreme circumstances may require the closing of the organization. In the event of such closings, the news outlets will be informed, and a message will be left on the organization's main phone number.

Solicitation

Volunteers and interns are not permitted to sell goods or distribute literature while exercising their responsibilities. A volunteer/intern may not solicit other volunteers/interns or an employee during the latter's working time. Volunteers must not solicit or distribute literature on the organization's premises.

Dress Code

Your clothing and grooming should be appropriate for a casual business environment. Do not wear clothing that may cause injury to yourself while completing your volunteer duties. This includes open-toed shoes, hanging earrings, long necklaces, large rings, scarves, or neckties. In some cases, health and safety standards may require special clothing, shoes, or hairstyles. In those cases, you are expected to comply with the company's requirements.

Signing In and Out

Please be sure to sign in and out at the volunteer desk when you start and end your shift. Obtain a volunteer badge from the desk upon your arrival. The badge should be worn at all times when you are on the organization's premises and returned to the desk when you leave.

ⓖ Volunteer Hour Logs and Sign-In Sheets

Samples of the volunteer hour logs, time sheets, and sign in sheets can be found in chapter 5, in the appropriate sections with individual (Table 5.2), teen (Table 5.1), student (Table 5.3), and children (Table 5.4) volunteers.

When writing job duty descriptions, include what needs to be done to complete the task so volunteers know what they are signing up for. This will also free up library staff to continue on with their daily work when volunteers come in, instead of having to stop and explain to volunteers what they are supposed to do and how. Here are a few examples:

Shelving Fiction Books. The volunteer will sign in and then go to the returned books shelving area to see what adult fiction books need to be shelved. The volunteer will pick two letter groups and alphabetize them on a book cart. They will take the cart to the adult fiction section and shelve the books in alphabetical order by author's last name. If there are any questions, please ask a library employee instead of shelving the books in a place that might be incorrect. If the volunteer completes the task before their shift is done, they can go back to the reshelving area to pick more books to shelve until all are shelved or their shift is done. The volunteer will then sign out and total their hours for the shift.

*This job description can be duplicated and slightly modified for fiction picture books, fiction children's books, and fiction young adult books, as well as movies, music, or anything else that might be shelved alphabetically.

Shelving Nonfiction Books. The volunteer will sign in and then go to the returned books shelving area to see what nonfiction books need to be shelved. The volunteer will pick one Dewey Decimal classification and put them in numerical order on a book cart. They will take the cart to the adult nonfiction section and shelve the books in numerical order according to the spine label. If there are any questions, please ask a library employee instead of shelving the books in a place that might be incorrect. If the volunteer completes the task before their shift is done, they can go back to the reshelving area to pick more books to shelve until all are shelved or their shift is done. At the end of their shift, the volunteer will sign out and total their hours for the shift.

*This job description can be duplicated and slightly modified for nonfiction children's books, reference books, or anything else that might be shelved according to the Dewey Decimal system.

Adults can help with programming if they have signed a liability form; if they are working with children, they might need a background check, but this is usually only required if they will be alone with children with no library employees present.

Programming Assistance. The volunteer will sign in half an hour before the program is to begin. They will go to the meeting room or storytime room, wherever the program is taking place, and assist the library employee with setting up the room. This includes moving tables and chairs, prepping supplies, and promoting the program to library patrons in the building. Once the program starts, the volunteer will stay in the room and act as a second set of hands for the library employee, handing out supplies, assisting patrons who need help, and more. The volunteer will help the program finish at the set time and stay behind to clean up with the library employee. The volunteer will sign out and total their shift hours after the program has completely wrapped up.

*This volunteer description can be edited to be more specific about a certain program, especially if it requires special skills or talents. It can also be revised to be a more general description that encompasses a series of programs that would benefit from having a consistent volunteer, like during the summer.

Tech Support. The volunteer helps patrons working on public library computers with various technical tasks. No task should include the patron giving or the volunteer asking for personal information. Help logging on and printing is a priority. The volunteer is able to clear paper jams from the library printer and restock printer paper. The volunteer can walk around the library wearing a Tech Support badge until a patron needs help or a computer has an issue. If the volunteer is willing, it can also be arranged that patrons can sign up for short IT Help sessions with the volunteer. This will be a one-on-one session where the patron can bring their own device to get help with using it, or get more involved help on a library public computer.

ⓖ Promotional Material Ideas

Think outside of the box when it comes to promotional materials. An ad on the library website is always a good idea and can be changed relatively easily. For paper promotional materials, think of things that will stick with potential volunteers. A bookmark is a great choice for a library—it is useful, informative, and practical. Patrons might grab one because they need a bookmark, then read it over and learn about the library's volunteer programs. Circulation staff can even automatically put a bookmark in one of every patron's checked out books.

Adding a brief line about the volunteer program on other program flyers can also be an effective way of marketing. Whether the library puts out a larger flyer of the month's children's, teens', and adults' programming or makes individual flyers for each program, there can be room to put a line about volunteer opportunities, and a link to the online application or directing patrons to paper applications kept at the desk.

If the library is involved with community outreach, the bookmarks would still be a memorable way to promote the volunteer program while putting the library at the forefront of potential patrons' minds. It is also a good idea to keep flyers on the smaller side; large pieces of paper get folded up, tucked away, and forgotten about. One innovative idea is to use an 8.5" x 11" sheet of paper to print two flyers lengthwise. These flyers can be folded into fourths to be business card sized, which is something people are used to taking and putting in their pockets to look at later. This design allows for different folding options: brochure fold, or with the outermost panels folded in so they unfold into a larger image space that can hold more information about the volunteer program.

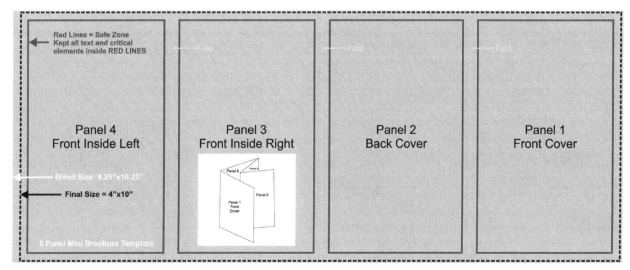

Figure 7.1. Template to create a small volunteer program brochure that folds up to the size of a business card.

If the library does not have an in-house printing department, high quality printers, or the budget to get materials printed, turn to the Internet. Design digital flyers, banners, and badges easily through sites like Canva—it's a free site that has attractive templates ready to go. Insert the library's volunteer program information, save the graphics, and post them on the library's website, Facebook page, and other social media outlets. Creating designs on Canva can even be outsourced to volunteers, as long as library employees still have a final look at the graphic before it is publicly shared.

Key Points

- Volunteer applications can be simple and straightforward, or slightly more detailed to give the volunteer coordinator more information up front.
- The volunteer handbook will have a lot of information that volunteers need to know, but if the library cannot print copies for all volunteers, find a place to keep it on the library website so it can be accessed any time the volunteer needs information.
- Job descriptions should be detailed and give a lot of information about the task overall, and steps on how to complete it.
- Volunteers can help refine their job descriptions and create new ones as more jobs are created.
- Promotional materials should be attention-getting, so be picky with the colors and fonts chosen to represent the library's volunteer program.
- Bookmarks are a great way for the library to promote their volunteer program, because everyone needs a bookmark!
- Promotional materials do not have to be printed—online banners and ads are just as effective at getting attention!

Bibliography

"CARDS." Military Missions—Supporting Active Military and Veterans. Accessed July 10, 2018. https://military-missions.org/care-packages/cards/.

Cards and Letters for Military. Accessed July 10, 2018. http://www.operationwearehere.com/IdeasforSoldiersCardsLetters.html.

"Cards for Hospitalized Kids." Cards for Hospitalized Kids. Accessed July 10, 2018. http://www.cardsforhospitalizedkids.com/.

"Cards Plus Team." Soldiers' Angels—Cards Plus Team. Accessed July 10, 2018. https://soldiersangels.org/cards-plus-team.html.

"Create Greeting Cards." Doing Good Together™. Accessed July 10, 2018. https://www.doinggoodtogether.org/bhf/create-greeting-cards/.

"From Project to Branch Integration and Sustainability: Community-Led Work at Halifax Public Libraries." Public Libraries Online. Accessed May 9, 2018. http://publiclibrariesonline.org/2013/04/from-project-to-branch-integration-and-sustainability-community-led-work-at-halifax-public-libraries/.

GivePulse.com. "Volunteer and Make A Difference Today | Volunteer Odyssey." GivePulse. Accessed June 14, 2018. https://serve.volunteerodyssey.com/.

Hasheck, Karen. "Send A Smile 4 Kids." Send A Smile 4 Kids. Accessed July 10, 2018. https://sendasmile4kids.blogspot.com/.

"Interview with Sarah Petschonek." Email interview by author. July 20, 2018.

"Interview with Stephen Ashley." Email interview by author. July 16, 2018.

Johnson, Abby. "Helping Hands: Libraries Connect Kids with Volunteer Opportunities." *American Libraries*, May 2018, 56.

"LRNG | About." LRNG. Accessed May 24, 2018. https://www.lrng.org/about.

McCurley, Stephen, and Rick Lynch. *Volunteer Management: Mobilizing All the Resources in the Community*. Downers Grove, IL: Heritage Arts Publishing, 1996.

"Personalized Children's Books." Letters of Love. Accessed July 10, 2018. https://www.iseeme.com/en-us/letters-of-love.html.

"Play Online, Learn Online and Feed the Hungry." Freerice.com | Not Your Average Online Trivia Game. Accessed September 3, 2018. http://freerice.com/.

"Read for Goats Winter Reading Challenge." Cedar Mill & Bethany Community Libraries. December 19, 2017. Accessed September 3, 2018. https://library.cedarmill.org/kids/read-for-goats-winter-reading-challenge-for-kids/.

"Send a Greeting Card." Nationwide Children's Hospital. Accessed July 10, 2018. https://www.nationwidechildrens.org/greeting-card.

"Send a Letter." A Million Thanks—Send a Letter. Accessed July 10, 2018. http://amillionthanks
.org/send_a_letter.php.

"What Is the Monetary Value of Volunteer Time? | Knowledge Base." GrantSpace. Accessed
August 1, 2019. http://www.grantspace.org/resources/knowledge-base/monetary-value-of
-volunteer-time/.

"Write Letters." Operation Gratitude. Accessed July 10, 2018. https://www.operationgratitude
.com/express-your-thanks/write-letters/.

Index

About the Author

Allison Renner began volunteering as a child and has been amazed at the doors volunteering has opened for her. She volunteered with SRVS, a nonprofit organization that provides services to people with disabilities. Her dedication led to the organization hiring her as the first volunteer coordinator, where she created a volunteer program from scratch. She volunteered with Memphis Public Libraries, which led to a position as the teen services librarian of a large branch within the system. Along with her regular job duties, she was also in charge of teen volunteers. She volunteered as a blogger for YALSAblog, and after a year was appointed member manager. Allison, along with six other YALSA members, wrote the Teen Literacies Toolkit for YALSA, which is an accessible handbook for library staff to use on the job. She earned her master of library science from Texas Woman's University, and also has a bachelor of arts in English, and an associate of applied science in graphic design. Allison has also worked as an elementary school librarian, and is currently a MakerSpace librarian at a Montessori school.